For Rebecca David,

Wishing you Bliss

Paul Taylor

# Capturing the Bliss

*Ayurveda and the Yoga of Emotion*

## Paul Dugliss, M.D.

No part of this book is to be taken as a substitute for medical advice. Consult your health-care provider before making or implementing any changes based on this book.

Cover Design: Ko Wicke, Proglyphics, Royal Oak, MI.

# TABLE OF CONTENTS

*Dedicated to the Divinity in you.*

# *1*

# AN OUTRAGEOUS BOOK

This is a totally outrageous book. To suggest that the ever-present experience of bliss can become a living reality is just pure fantasy for most. A book based on such a premise is simply too far out. Suggesting that bliss can be a daily experience is completely contrary to most people's lives. It would seem that a book based on that principle is doomed to end up in the circular file. But here it is, and here you are because something in your heart knows better. Some part of you knows that there is more to life than what you may have been told.

No apologies for this book will be offered. The inside secret is that the design for the human being endows each person with the tremendous potential for experiencing how each emotion can lead to the state of bliss. In the hidden tangle of "modern education," the most important aspects of being human are left out. We graduate without an understanding of who we are and of what we are capable. Because it is inherent in our nature, the idea of bliss appeals to us. Your heart knows. It senses the capability and is willing to suggest to your mind that you entertain this outrageous book — maybe, just a bit further...

If your education did not include a course on love, then a book on bliss might be necessary. If your education did not include a course on emotion, then a book that describes the design for human emotion might be in order. If you have not learned how to transform emotion into bliss, then a new knowledge is needed. Where to find this knowledge? No technical manual exists. Nothing on the Internet offers a guide. Where is this knowledge that is akin to wisdom? Where to turn? Where to look?

The ancients knew this wisdom. The wisdom of the East contains this knowledge. The medicines of the East had to understand this, because they understood the great impact of emotion on health. The sage-physicians understood that health and emotion are intimately intertwined. They designed ways of treating disease from the inside out and provided us with the secrets to living bliss 24 hours a day.

This book is about those secrets. It is about a science of life called Ayurveda that provides the secrets of how emotions work. While commonly thought to be "Indian herbal medicine," Ayurveda comes from two Sanskrit words: *Ayur* meaning life and *Veda* meaning truth. Any medical system that claims to know the truth of life must have a deep understanding of mind-body interactions and emotions. Ayurveda does. Furthermore, it understands the full potential we humans possess.

Much of what comes out of the East is initially seen as outrageous. When the British first saw Ayurvedic physicians using herbalized oils on the skin in the 19th century, they scoffed. They thought it was preposterous that any of the herb could travel through the thick layer of skin into the body. Medical science now knows that the skin becomes porous in the presence of oily substances, and the transdermal patch which allows medicine to be delivered through the skin is the result. What was once outrageous, when understood, becomes completely useful.

In entertaining the preposterousness of bliss, we come to know that area of our hearts that lies deepest and most protected. We come to know possibilities only heretofore dreamt of. We come to an understanding of our innermost workings. And we learn about the essence of love, of life and of the wonders of the human experience. Being one with the secret nature of bliss, we can go from the outrageous to the possible.

The secrets of Ayurveda are the secrets of life itself. Ayurveda holds the potential for infinite expansion and growth. The secrets of the heart and the innermost aspects of our beings are unfolded in this way, in this path, in this truth of life.

In knowledge is power — power to create, power to grow, power to evolve. In this education, we come to experience the secrets of the inner life — not just the mechanics of how biology works, but the knowledge of how *we* work inside.

Life is, for so many of us, so far from bliss. Depression is as frequent as the common cold. Anxiety is the daily experience of many. Frustration, anger and road rage are all too familiar. The boldness of a book on bliss is bolstered only by the experience of watching this transformation take place in patient after patient. Predictably, for one person after another, applying the principles of Ayurveda has led to a profound awakening of comfort, well-being, peace, joy and happiness. Bliss is the expression on their faces. Bliss is the signature of their treatments. Bliss is the result, time and time again.

If you are able to sit with your skepticism and not act on it just yet, what you will encounter in each chapter of this book is some of the reality the sages of the East experienced. You will find what you can do to apply this wisdom to your life, and most importantly, you will discover the impact it can have on your emotions, on how you feel.

We live life through our emotions. How we feel about something really determines everything — our attitude our thoughts, our actions. The feeling level of life is where the dynamic flow of liveliness and energy comes forth and imbues life with its excitement and awe. It is where motivation and drive originate. It is where the love resides that ties ow does one become a butterfly," she asked pensively. "n must want to fly so much that you are willing to give up being a caterpillar."

rough space and time. The emotional life
y and the flow upon which thoughts and

omeone well or find someone distasteful it
el that is at play. When we are excited to go
dreading another day at the job, it is the
of existence that determines our day. When
es drawn to that piece of chocolate, regard-
r minds say, it is the power of emotion that
inking.

tions originate? How do they get processed
d? Where do they flow? What happens that
be painful? In understanding the secrets of
nderstand the answer to these questions.

Ayurveda are now just coming out to the
ave been hidden for centuries. A complete
ge of life must offer knowledge of emotional life.
it does. This book is about those secrets. It is a guide-
for understanding the emotional life.

e limit of our awareness of the emotional field, we per-
so often in glimpses. And these overwhelm. Ann
es to my clinic because of its alternative focus. She has
diagnosed with breast cancer. It has been caught at the
est stage and she has undergone surgery and radiation
ments. Her doctors pronounced her cured. Yet, she
rs. She agonizes each day about whether the cancer
come back, what it will mean for her life, when she will

die, what effect it will have on her children and her family. She avoids the emotional field and tries to remain busy. When the pressure mounts, the fear rears up, and she is paralyzed. She glimpses the vastness of it and has to run away. Her fear hounds her. She calls her husband five times a day for reassurance that she heard accurately what the surgeon said. She is never at ease. She hears the words but never believes the positive prognosis.

Ann suffers tremendously, even though she is "cured." She has no means to cope and is put on antidepressant medications and tranquilizers by her psychiatrist. Yet the fear persists. She stops relating to others because she is afraid they may ask how she is doing.

Ann suffers because she has no way to metabolize her experience. She has no way to "digest" her fear and transform it and the energy behind it into anything useful. She has no ability to remain aware and discover what lies behind her fear. She becomes a slave to her emotions, rather than having them serve her. She is in the bondage of a terrible nightmare that can only be endured with dependency on drugs. Even then, the nightmare is only less intense but still present.

To speak to Ann about bliss is impossible. It is so far from her experience. But to present her with a way to experience bliss is not only possible, but of utmost necessity. Through a series of special massage and oil treatments, her frazzled nerves are brought into a state of deep relaxation where she begins to let go of the hold her fears have on her. Through deep meditation, she begins to experience the field of existence that underlies her feelings and supports them. She begins to contact a different place within herself. She begins to know herself in a different way. With special herbs she begins to wean herself off of the mind-numbing medications and begins to have periods when she can "be her old self" and enjoy life again. Finally, through understanding the Ayurvedic approach, she starts to allow her emotions to flow and change and transform as she becomes more clearly aware of her emotional field. The fears come, but they go just as quickly. They are manageable. And she begins to experience the bliss that underlies her existence.

This is the power of knowledge. This is medicine whose most potent treatment is wisdom. This is the possibility of bliss in the face of its most outrageous impossibility.

Most of us are like Ann. Life has left us so overwhelmed on the emotional level that we have little left to deal with it. Without any guideposts, without anything to light the way, we have no concept of bliss and its possibility. The grace of the ancient sages' wisdom sounds so far-fetched. And yet, here it is.

It is here because it is time. It is the time now for a way out of the suffering. It is time now for a new knowledge. It is time for the birthright of each of us to manifest in its full glory. It is time for bliss to become a common experience. This book is part of the answer to the need of this time. Its purpose is to ease the suffering and allow the bliss that underlies life to shine forth in each of our hearts. If you are led to this book, if you find yourself drawn to it, it is only because a deeper part of you knows that this wisdom can help you.

Wisdom is recognized by the heart as much as by the head. You are drawn to it because "the truth shall set you free." The yoga of emotion is the unity of bliss that underlies the experience of every emotion, every feeling. In the true meaning of yoga we have union. In that union we rest in the ocean where bliss resides. Wave upon wave of emotion flows up to the surface, is experienced and falls back into the ocean, into the bliss that is beneath all the flows. Wave upon wave of emotion comes crashing back into a sea of love that fills the heart. When we let love fill us, when we let bliss be ours in THIS moment, emotions do not stick to us. A fear comes up and falls back into love. A frustration tangles into itself and is dissolved. We put forth a desire, and we let the yoga guide its fulfillment. This is the yoga of emotion. This is the way of Ayurveda. This is the wisdom of emotion. And this is what this book is meant to lead you to...

## *2*

# OUTSTANDING IN YOUR FIELD

---

## *The Need of the Time*

Success comes to those who are outstanding in their fields. But there is another field of life in which each of us can excel, in which we can come to great success, to great happiness. That field lies deep within us. Understanding that field requires a way of exploring inward. It requires us knowing ourselves in a complete way. In understanding this inner dimension, we find all outer glories. It is the paradox of wisdom. By going deep within, we can create better on the outside. By retiring, we create success in all of life. Being glorious in this inner space requires practice, technique and a modicum of faith. But it is more than an abstract possibility.

For many there is a knowing — a sense of something more. Thought, emotion, the practicalities of life, relationships all blend to cloud the inner treasures. Yet through the clouds we catch a glimpse occasionally of something more. In our hearts we know that life is clearly not about what is outside of us. Yet how to explore what is inside? Talk therapy rarely gets at the subconscious mind. What lies beyond the subconscious? Inner space is so deep. What is the field that underlies the subconscious?

The need is to find a way of exploring inner space. By exploring that something more we find the source of thought, the source of happiness and bliss. We find a stability. It only requires a way of exploring.

## Patty — Picture of Sadness

Patty comes to my office and is asked if she minds if a medical student is present while we talk. She does not mind and we begin to talk. She is barely understandable; she talks so quietly. She quit her job as a respiratory therapist because she is severely depressed. She cries on and off through much of the interview. Her psychiatrist has tried her on several medications. She is currently on two antidepressants and one antipsychotic medication. Barely able to hold her head up, she complains, "I do not like these medications. I have gained 20 pounds since going on the antipsychotic." She cannot make eye contact with either me or my student.

I ask the medical student to leave the interview after a short while, hoping this will make her feel more comfortable, but it does not help in the least. Patty describes how happy she used to be. She is married and has two children. She had difficulties with an overly demanding father when she was growing up, but outside of working through those issues, has been generally happy. "Everything was going well. My job, my kids..." She cannot understand what happened to her life.

"The hospital was running into financial difficulty, and I had to go back to working nights. That is when everything seemed to fall apart. I had just been off for six weeks maternity leave and came back to work, and two months later everything fell apart. I am worried now that my husband will leave me..."

Patty's depression is severe and long-standing. I discuss with her the Ayurvedic approach to treating depression. We talk about daily routine. I suggest we hold off on herbal therapy until I can research interactions between her antipsychotic medication and herbs. As part of her treatment I suggest we consider a way of gaining deep rest — a way of contacting the inner depths of herself. I suggest a specific form of meditation and caution her that nonpharmacological approaches take time. I assure her that she will benefit, but that she may not notice much before our next appointment.

## *What She Doesn't Understand*

Patty doesn't understand how she can still be depressed in spite of everything: the drugs, the great family, her wonderful husband, her beautiful children, her high-paying job. She cannot comprehend why she doesn't feel well. She is fed up with trying one new drug after another, only to encounter more side effects.

What Patty doesn't understand is who she really is, where her energy comes from, where her liveliness originates. She does not understand the role of awareness in her existence. She does not understand how her unique individuality requires a different routine, a different diet and a unique way of nurturing herself that only she can discover by developing her awareness. She does not understand her life force and how she has depleted it.

Trapped in the idea of biochemistry, she views her depression as a biochemical imbalance. She relies on the use of external supplementation to replenish her depleted brain. She does not understand that the brain supports her awareness but does not create it. Drugs can never change her internal workings.

Patty is lost in the overwhelming barrage of thoughts and feelings that completely consume her experience. She has little peace or silence and no awareness or experience of her consciousness *as separate from her thoughts and feelings*. She is totally bound and totally involved in the conundrum that has become her life. Bliss is the farthest thing from her mind. She would be happy just to be suffering less.

Scientists continue to explore outer space. In exploring inner space, though, we have the key to solving the riddle of depression. Inner space is as vast and complex and as full of beautiful stars and amazing planets as is outer space. In opening to the possibility of what resides within, we are boldly led to discover the meaning of our lives. Without turning inward we lose the keys to the kingdom, as it were. Wandering with no money, we have forgotten how to go to the bank, how to withdraw money and live a life of fullness, happiness and wealth.

## What Ayurveda Understands

The most fundamental understanding of Ayurveda is that all of life, all of creation arises from an underlying field of energy and intelligence. Out of this field of Absolute energy, bliss and creativity, all aspects of material existence are formed. And out of this field all thought and emotion arise. The ancients described this field as one of pure bliss consciousness. They provided techniques of deep meditation in which thought is transcended, and one is able to experience this field directly. Recently, the field of physics has discovered solutions to Einstein's quest for a unified field theory. The descriptions of the Unified Field in physics correlate perfectly with what the ancients described.

## *The Unified Field?*

The Unified Field is what the ancients referred to as the Absolute. It is the sum total of all energy and potentials — all creativity and all intelligence. When it stirs within itself, it creates the relative, manifested creation. When we use the term "relative" we mean that something has manifested out of the Unified Field that no longer demonstrates all the qualities of the Absolute and can be known by comparing it relative to other aspects of creation. A red flower is soft compared to a hardwood floor, and we know red when we compare it to pink and yellow and the other colors. We know the floor's hardness is relative in terms of existence, in terms of time. It comes and goes, and change is the only constant of the relative field.

How then do you describe the Absolute, which is the sum total of all qualities? How do you describe the indescribable? Words only hint at it. The ancients called it *sat chit ananda*. Translated, *sat* means pure, *chit* means consciousness, and *ananda* means bliss. The Absolute is pure bliss consciousness. When pure bliss consciousness moves, it is pure love and out of this movement, creation is born. Love is sat chit ananda in motion. It is pure e-motion, as it is the movement of the Absolute. This motion of the Absolute creates the attracting power of love.

Everything that flows out of the Absolute eventually flows back into it, and this flow creates love. That is its start and that is its endpoint. Every emotion is a stir in the field of consciousness, and every emotion flows (if we let it) and brings us back to the Absolute, back to the love out of which all emotion is born. From love to love is the normal natural course of emotion. We are trained very early on in life to interfere with the normal flow — that certain feelings and ways of expressing are not acceptable — and the natural process is distorted. We do not know who we are. We do not know where emotion starts. We intertwine emotion with our being and let it overshadow our awareness and become lost in relative creation. In this darkness love cannot shine. Emotion does not flow. We are lost as to how emotion can return to love and bliss.

Ayurveda is about what is natural. It is about how Nature works and how experience is metabolized. It is about the normal function and process of being human. Most importantly, it is about the Absolute. Charak, the ancient sage physician who first codified the sayings of Ayurveda thousands of years ago, stated:

*Mind, soul, and body, this trinity called the human being, rests on Unity like a tripod. Upon that Unified Field everything rests. That Purusha or Absolute Being is also animate and is regarded as the subject matter of the science of Ayurveda. It is also for the sake of Unity with that Absolute that this science is promulgated.*

Ultimately, that Unified Field, being a field of bliss and love, is the source of true happiness. In coming into harmony with that, we fulfill the main purpose of Ayurveda, the expansion of happiness.

## If Expansion of Happiness is the Purpose of Life, Why Doesn't it Feel That Way?

True happiness is when we sit in the bliss of Being, when we are able to be in direct contact with the source of life, with our liveliness. Happiness is not the result of success. It is the result of developing awareness, of developing consciousness, and through this development establishing a direct connection with the Absolute.

When we come into this present moment, when we drop the commentary on our experience, we come into Being and create the potential for experiencing true happiness. When we are pulled away from this moment, when we lose awareness of our being, then happiness is elusive.

Ayurveda understands that the root cause of suffering is our becoming disconnected from Nature, from the Unified Field. Through our free will we can choose to do things that pull us away from Nature and from our true nature. In this process of disharmony, we create habits that disconnect us and create disintegration. Our experience, our awareness becomes clouded with thought, emotion and the impression of the senses, and we lose all awareness of the underlying being. In this state, happiness is lost or is only a fleeting experience when a desire is fulfilled. Trapped in that state of limited awareness, the mind searches aimlessly after anything that will give some modicum of pleasure. We chase our desires into the world, hoping that once they are fulfilled we will be satisfied. But it is a bottomless pit, because once a desire is fulfilled, another arises and with it the illusion that we must chase after this next thing in order to be truly happy.

Ayurveda understands that desires are a part of life and that it is natural to want them to be fulfilled. But the happiness we experience when they are fulfilled is just our momentary letting go and experiencing the bliss of existence — that life is good. Fulfilling desires taps us into the underlying field of bliss because it is our nature to want to fulfill desires. But how much more direct is it to go directly to the field of bliss and not have to wait for our desires to be fulfilled? This is done through deep meditation, which is not a part of our culture or our education. Hence, to talk of bliss and the expansion of happiness is so far from the daily experience that it sounds hokey.

So much of our unhappiness comes in not understanding life. Life is the precious flow of consciousness and awareness. When we stop this flow or diminish it, suffering results. To be in the flow of pure awareness and to observe the emotions is the Ayurvedic prescription for a healthy emotional life. The yoga of emotion is this uniting with the field of bliss and fully experiencing emotion simultaneously. *Yoga* means union. In union with the bliss of being, we allow emotion to flow like a wave on an ocean and find it makes us swell up and come merging once again with the source of happiness.

## A Really Huge Diet

In what we see, hear, touch, taste, smell, think and feel we re-create ourselves. The power of the Absolute, the Unified Field, is in its creative capability. It is like water on a garden — whichever part you water grows. It is the power of our awareness. Whatever we put our attention on, grows and creates. Each sense brings with it associations that reverberate in our emotional sphere and pulls us out of the blissful peace into the play of emotion. Each emotion has its moment on the stage and then is ready to fall back into the silent ocean of bliss.

## Who We Are

Ayurveda has this profound understanding of who we are. Rather than seeing the body as a complex machine that has somehow learned to think, Ayurveda understands that we are nonmaterial beings who create our bodies. This uncanny and uncommon notion has its roots in a wisdom that has been lost and is now being regained.

Wisdom is a realm frequented as often by poets and musicians as it is by scientists. An allegory portrays the understanding of Ayurveda: One day the emperor of a vast kingdom decides he wants to understand the life of his subjects. He dons the clothes of a commoner and sneaks out of his castle into the village. Wandering into the village he takes a fall and bumps his head, knocking himself out. On coming to, he has amnesia. He forgets that he is the emperor and ruler of all he surveys. He wanders about in the village and talks with the people and is taken in by a kind family. He helps by doing menial labor — sweeping and cleaning, chopping wood and tending the garden for the family. Having lost his memory, his clarity of mind, he has lost his status as ruler. His life is now controlled by those around him, by the weather that affects his garden and by the gossip that fills the community.

One day his ministers and assistants come scouring the village to see if they can find their lost leader. When they discover him tending the garden of the family, they are shocked. They tell him that he must come back now to claim his rightful role as leader. He does not believe them. It seems so far-fetched for a lowly gardener to be considered a king. He begs them to stop leading him on and to let him get back to his gardening. No amount of convincing by his ministers can turn the gardener back into the king.

In Ayurveda when the body's intelligence is blocked from manifesting as it was designed, it is said to have "lost its memory" or *Smriti* value. Without proper memory of the design, the system fails. Healing is said to be a matter of re-establishing the Smriti of the body, the body's memory of how to function perfectly. Likewise, the king needs to remember and eventually recognizes the faces of his ministers and realizes they are right. He is the king. Ayurveda restores complete memory — cellular memory, physical memory, psychological and spiritual memory are all restored. In this process, wholeness is returned. In this process, we remember *who we really are.*

The potential we hold within is unfathomable. We barely give grace to that which is within, because we have not been shown the way to tap into the huge reservoir of energy and intelligence. In the absence of this light of knowledge, darkness takes over and we assume that practical life is all that human existence is made of. In this cultural delusion, we become lost.

Our experience is just that of the king. The "knock on the head" that we receive is an uncultivated potential. The normal growth and integration of the nervous system is halted in adolescence for most people, due to a lack of proper development of consciousness. We are overwhelmed by the senses and thoughts and feelings that move on the landscape of consciousness, so much so that we are unaware of its nature. We live under the illusion that we are the thoughts, we are the personality, we are the feelings, rather than that which experiences thoughts and feelings. We lose our divinity and become trapped in the illusion that we are the body. We think we exist as a brain wrapped in skin. We too often feel we end where the body ends. We view ourselves like an egg. We have an outer shell that contains all of who we are. We end at the shell and try to hide from the outside world all the soft mushy stuff inside.

## The Inside Scoop — We are Nonmaterial Beings

Ask most people who they are, and they give you their name. Ask who that person is that the name refers to, and many will point to the body. In the grand scheme of any given life, the body is really a very fleeting event. If you have the concept that you *are* your body, that your cells have somehow gotten together and created a mind, then you were not here a year ago. Here is the physical story:

- 98% of the molecules that make up the body are replaced in one year's time.

- The lining of the stomach replaces itself in five days.

- Liver cells are constantly being destroyed and replaced. Cut off a lobe of the liver and it can replace itself in two months. The entire liver is replaced in six months.

- Even the most solid parts of us, our bones, are replaced continuously. Bone is constantly being reabsorbed and rebuilt, and if there is an imbalance in the process, osteoporosis is the result.

If you think you are the body, then what you saw in the mirror this morning was not there a year ago. The body has been almost entirely replaced. Even brain cells are constantly being restructured. While thought not to regenerate, brain cells are constantly replacing their internal structure, if not creating new dendrites and losing old ones. The body is impermanent, yet we persist. As kings and queens, our "knock on the head" creates the illusion that we are the body.

Another way to this understanding is knowledge of human memory. The human brain contains approximately 100 billion neurons. This seems like a huge number, yet we know these cells are organized by function. The cells at the back of the brain, for example, relate to visual functions and sight. Large areas of the brain provide for movement and balance. Even if the entire brain were utilized for memory, it would not be sufficient to store all the data accessed by an average person.

If memories were stored in brain cells, even with the most sophisticated compression scheme, when you reached the point of seeing more than 50 movies there would be no storage left in the brain. Of course, most people don't recall all the scenes of a movie. However, research has shown that when prompted, most can retrieve the memory of any given scene. Take the movie *Titanic* with Kate Winslet and Leonardo DiCaprio. Since the movie was popular many years ago, most will not be able to recall much about the film. If prompted, however, many will be able to recall when Leonardo DiCaprio takes Kate Winslet up to the bow of the boat, without her being able to see, and then asks her to open her eyes.

If one can be prompted to recall, then the memory must be there. Rather than holding just 50 movies, the brain can hold hundreds of movies, hundreds of books, thousands of words of vocabulary, multiple languages, images, thoughts, feelings, memories. If memory were limited to the brain cells, it would get "full" and you would start losing older information like your name and what your parents looked like. This, obviously, does not occur. If there are simply too few cells in the brain to store all the information, where is it stored?

## The Underlying Field

The ever-changing nature of the body and the concept of the brain as being insufficient to contain all our memories challenges any notion that we are just physical beings. The brain cannot be a complex computer that stores and creates thoughts. Instead, the brain is like an amplifier in a radio. You tune into a certain station (a certain thought), and this is amplified (brought to awareness).

If we are just some energy in some field, why do we have the sense of being isolated and separate from other people? Why can't others tap into our memories? Actually, some psychics can to some extent, and here is why. Imagine a large pool with a wave machine. Over the pool you lay a fishnet. Suppose the fishnet was lined with a special refrigerating device that could instantly freeze the water above the net, while leaving the water below it liquid. Let us do an experiment. We place the net a foot above the surface level of the pool so that only the very crests of the tall waves are above the net and are instantly frozen. What happens? We are left with a set of individual crests, each unique.

Suppose each crest could be animated with a personality and awareness. One crest would look out and see other crests, each unique, each individual and separate. Now let's do the same experiment but lower the level of the net. We then end up with each "crest" having greater depth, more awareness of what is at its base. Eventually, if we lower the level of the net sufficiently into the pool, each wave connects to the others through the water from which they arise. The level of the net corresponds with the "level" of awareness of the underlying field, of the Absolute.

Suppose an individual wave named Fred becomes aware of the underlying pool of water and starts to sense some of the smaller flows and vibration that are affecting the next crest over. Suddenly, Fred is able to get some impressions of what his fellow wave is experiencing. Fred has become a "psychic" wave.

In this manner, we are individual beings, nonmaterial and independent, yet connected. We are all part of the same pool, the same ocean. What is the water? The water is consciousness. Our awareness or consciousness is connected to a sea of consciousness. That sea contains tremendous energy, information and intelligence. It must be so, as we are intelligent beings, and we come out of it.

Human beings are described in Ayurvedic medicine as consciousness made manifest. Consciousness can be thought of in terms of an energy, like electricity or light, but it is much more than that. It contains intelligence, organization and creativity. It is the creative force that underlies creation.

At the base of the sea of consciousness, there are no waves, just stillness. On the surface, waves and vibrations form. Like any vibration these are composed of different frequencies. The human physiology is essentially designed for the transformation of these various frequencies to create the thoughts, feelings and the energy that inform our physical being, as well as our awareness of them.

Consciousness is like white light and the human being is like a prism. We transform energy and create various colors through various energy centers in the body. Like electricity, consciousness comes from a source, a power plant. The energy coming from an electrical power plant is at 100,000 volts — enough power to fry any electrical device in your home. At a substation the voltage is down-regulated to 10,000 volts and at the line to the house to 240 volts, and in the house to 120, and then in some devices (like computers) to just 6 volts. Just like this, the energy of the Absolute must be transformed so that the body can make use of it.

Like the power plant, consciousness at its source has tremendous power. Unlike electricity, though, it contains the fabric or template or intelligence for the many forms it inhabits. The various aspects of human existence (spirit, mind, emotions, body) are the expressions of various frequencies of the field of consciousness — just like the prism and the numerous frequencies of light that form different colors. One frequency or color corresponds to mental activity, one to emotional activity, one to the spiritual level. Our entire existence is organized around transforming these frequencies of consciousness into human experience.

## The First Three Secrets of Ayurveda

Ayurveda is really all about how consciousness works. Consciousness serves as the basis for emotion. Understanding it allows us to perceive new ways to deal with emotions. Three key principles of Ayurveda in regard to the workings of consciousness are:

Contacting the underlying field, the Absolute, and reconnecting with the underlying sea of consciousness at the base of human existence reconnects the person with wholeness out of which everything comes. It re-creates health. Whenever the flow of consciousness and its intelligence and energy are blocked, the potential for disorganization, disease, pain and suffering is created.

Consciousness is a creative force — as in a garden — the area that is watered grows. Whatever we put our awareness on grows. Whatever we attend to gets animated and enlivened.

Think of consciousness as "life force" or "spirit." Wherever you invest your life force, liveliness is created. The more consciousness or life force, the more powerful the ability to create.

Another secret understood in Ayurveda is that the template for the proper unfolding of the physiology and the tissues exists like a design blueprint in consciousness. When the construction foreman loses the blueprints and cannot call the architect for a backup set of instructions, the construction project is likely to fail. It is the frictionless flow of energy and intelligence that takes place through the transformations of consciousness that allows health to be maintained. That is why the process does not involve will or effort. It is preprogrammed into the nature of the human being to transform consciousness into matter and into human experience.

The various levels of existence — spiritual, mental, emotional, etheric (the energy level that feeds the physical) and physical — are not simply concepts about different things that take place in one's head. They are actual fields, like levels in the ocean. They differ in the frequency of vibration. This is why one can be thinking one thing and feeling another. "I am not angry!" the supervisor yells. Mentally, the supervisor taps into one area; emotionally, quite another area of existence. Unfortunately, when these levels are not integrated, the result can be dysfunction.

The degree to which these areas of life are in contact with their source in the ocean of consciousness is the degree to which they are lively, vibrant and healthy. The more we disconnect from the source, the more fragmented, the less whole and healthy we become.

## The Flow

Seven consciousness/energy transformers exist in the human physiology. They are each associated with different vibrations, functions and psychospiritual knowledge. All of our human memories and experiences are organized around these energy/information centers. Those who have studied yoga will know these as *chakras*. They are sometimes referred to as the seven lotuses in Buddhist thought. They are described in terms of location, level of vibration of consciousness, psychology and physiology. On a physical level, they each relate to one of the endocrine organs in the body. A brief overview of the chakras is given in the table on the following page.

# The Chakras — An Overview

| | Name Location | Major Function | Emotional Complex | Divine Qualities Required |
|---|---|---|---|---|
| 1 | Muladhara (Root) <br><br> Base of the Spine | **Physical Identity – Security and sense of belonging.** Stores our tribal experience and memory – our cultural heritage and upbringing and our sense of belonging in a community. <br>**Self-Identity** | *Core:* Fear <br><br> *Related:* Holding On/ Controlling | Divine Faith: Letting Go, Letting God |
| 2 | Swadhisthana (Sweetness) <br><br> Lower Abdomen | **Emotional Identity – Emotions, the feeling sense and one-on-one relationships.** Stores our memories and experiences in close relationships of all kinds, including sexual experiences. <br>**Self-Gratification** | *Core:* Attachment <br><br> *Related:* Attachment to things rather than people | Divine Freedom, Divine Flow, Divine Pleasure |
| 3 | Manipura (Lustrous Gem) <br><br> Solar Plexus | **Ego Identity – Self-esteem and sense of autonomy.** Stores our memories and experiences related to our independence, our ability to achieve in the world and our sense of personal competence or power. <br>**Self-Definition** | *Core:* Low Self-esteem <br><br> *Related:* Competitive-ness, Egoism, Irritability, Anger | Divine Worth |

| | Name<br>Location | Major Function | Emotional<br>Complex | Divine<br>Qualities<br>Required |
|---|---|---|---|---|
| 4 | Anahata<br>(Unstruck)<br><br>Mid-sternum<br>(Heart) | **Social Identity –**<br>**Benevolent and**<br>**Divine Love.** Stores<br>our memories of love<br>and of our connection<br>to the Divine.<br>**Self-Acceptance** | *Core:* Hurt<br><br>*Related:* Self-<br>protective,<br>unemotional | Divine<br>Love,<br>Self-love as<br>a child of<br>the Divine |
| 5 | Vissudha<br>(Purification)<br><br>Throat | **Creative Identity –**<br>**Will to create and to**<br>**express.** Stores our<br>memories and<br>experience of<br>speaking up and<br>speaking out with our<br>creativity and our will<br>to create.<br>**Self-Expression** | *Core:*<br>Unassertive-<br>ness | Divine Will,<br>Divine<br>Power |
| 6 | Ajna (To<br>Perceive and<br>Command)<br><br>Forehead | **Archetypal Identity**<br>**– Ability to perceive.**<br>Stores our patterns of<br>perception and our<br>intuition – our ability<br>to know on a subtle<br>level and to know the<br>archetypal pattern we<br>are manifesting.<br>**Self-Reflection** | *Core:* Over-<br>intellectualiz-<br>ing | Divine<br>Intuition,<br>Divine<br>Knowing |
| 7 | Sahasrara<br>(Thousand-<br>Fold)<br><br>Crown of<br>Head | **Universal Identity –**<br>**Connection with the**<br>**Divine Truth.**<br>Houses our<br>connection to Spirit<br>and to Universal<br>Truth.<br>**Self-Knowledge** | *Core:* Denial,<br>particularly of<br>spiritual<br>development | Divine<br>Conscious-<br>ness |

All memory, all thoughts, each experience, each feeling makes an impression and an impact on one or more of the centers. Emotional experiences and connections to other people are stored in the chakras. Cellular memory stores these in the physical body. Consciousness stores these in the subtle body or higher frequencies of consciousness associated with each chakra.

The flow of consciousness starts at the Absolute, where the frequency of vibration is so high it is immeasurable (hence the name Absolute). It flows into the next levels, down each of the chakras, all the way down to the base of the physical level. Any blockage in its flow can create problems. Knowing on which level the blockage occurs and how to rebalance it is one of the key components of Ayurvedic medicine.

Not every blockage is a psychological issue or a spiritual one. Put a poison in your body, and the problem is not on the psychological level. It cannot be solved by positive thinking or resolving blockages to spiritual power. The unbridled enthusiasm that accompanied the discovery of mind-body medicine led too many people to believe they could heal anything just by changing their minds. Ayurveda recognizes that disease can arise on many levels and that the wise healer addresses the root cause. This means addressing problems on the appropriate level.

## The Ayurvedic Understanding: The Heart Knows the Connection Between Us

This has been an abstract understanding. On the level of the heart, we experience the truth of an underlying field. In lecturing about Ayurveda I often like to do a little survey to help people dispel the notion of the egg model. I ask them if they have ever reached out for the phone to dial a friend when the phone rang, and it was the person they intended to call. Think about this. What are the odds? There are 60 seconds in a minute, 60 minutes in an hour, 24 hours in a day, and you have probably at least 20 to 30 contacts that you call occasionally. That puts the odds in the lottery-winning range — about 1 in 1,724,800. Generally, when I ask how many have experienced this, anywhere from a third to the entire class say they have. I then ask how many have experienced winning a million dollars in the lottery. Honestly, I have never had a lottery winner in any of my classes.

This mechanism by which the friend knows to call necessitates that who we are does not end with the outline of our skin. We are connected at a more fundamental level than the physical body. A more appropriate way of thinking about this is to consider each of us as a wave on an underlying ocean of energy. Because of our limited awareness of the depths and currents of the ocean, we are only aware of what is on the surface. We look out and see individual waves — individual people — and assume there is no connection between them. If we develop our awareness more, then we are able to dive deeper into the depths of the ocean.

On the level of the heart we know this. We feel each other's pain. We feel the quality of the home they live in, even if they are not present. The heart knows the connection between us. It knows that we are deeply connected.

## Patty's Progress

Patty learned a meditation technique called Transcendental Meditation. She also implemented some of the lifestyle changes I recommended. As she was so depressed, I wanted to see her back in 10 days to confirm that she was making progress. "Patty is in Room 7," I told the medical school student when she came back for her return visit. "Why don't you say hello to her while I finish with this person." Ten minutes later I went to Room 7 and knocked on the door: "Could I interrupt and have a word with my medical student? I will be right with you, Patty." I then asked the medical student for her impressions and if she thought that anything had changed over the last 10 days.

The student answered, "I literally did not recognize her. I thought I was in the wrong room. She is smiling, making eye contact. This is unbelievable. How can I learn this meditation practice?" This medical student had the precious opportunity of observing how profound meditation can be. Patty was no longer depressed, was sleeping better, was beginning to function well with her family and had started taking on more responsibilities around the house. She was already talking about wanting to go back to work part time.

This is the power of reconnecting with the source of energy and intelligence.

## The Mind's Connection

To summarize this chapter, remember these three keys, or imperatives, from our understanding of consciousness:

The first is that reconnecting with the source of health — the power source or the pure consciousness that lies deep below the subconscious mind — is vital to the process of healing and maintaining health. In emotional terms, this means that proper mood is dependent on a strong life force, which comes from a strong connection to the Absolute.

The second imperative is that frictionless flow of consciousness/energy to the physical must be maintained for health to be optimal. Any blockage on any level can hamper the flow of intelligence and energy necessary for natural healing. Emotional blocks can hamper energy, physical health, but most importantly can block connection to the experience of the underlying bliss of the Absolute.

The third imperative originates in the principle that awareness or consciousness can animate and enliven anything. That means our awareness must attend to that which is in tune with our higher nature. Whatever we attend to grows. If we attend to a complex of having been wronged and ponder all the reasons we are justified in feeling so, then we actually create this in our lives. We create not only the opportunity to be wronged again, but more importantly we re-create the emotions we experienced in the past when we were wronged — *regardless of whether we have been wronged again.* This constant creation of emotional patterns produces an imbalance that blocks the normal flow of emotion, and the residual blocks the experience of bliss.

## *Heart to Heart — The Fulfillment*

The repeated contact with the source of life, with the Absolute, results in joy. Of this, what can be said? Not enough. The heart soars, and the rush of bliss rises forth in exuberance. The widening expansion of the heart unfolds. We revel in this land only so often. It brings forth such an intensity of feeling that each breath seems halted with the excitement of the rush. When joy meets its object, then the bliss of eternal Being is held in the awareness. A rushing surge of energy comes forth, and the fountainhead of creation serves its Creator. It serves the purpose of creation and in that it becomes the fulfillment for the heart, mind and soul. Each day that brings joy brings creation to its fulfillment. Live in that perfection. Be outstanding in that field. Capture the bliss...

## *Homework: Connect to the Source*

This is the most abstract discussion in this book. Without clear experience, contacting the Source can sound enigmatic. We conclude this chapter of the book with some practical exercises to bring home the key points.

We connect to the source in several ways. You can create the opportunity for experiencing the field of the Absolute. Among the mysteries of the king or queen who has lost his or her true identity is something as simple as sleep. Why do we sleep? What is the need? Medical science knows the need, but not the "why."

In transforming consciousness and energy into the physical body, we act as transformers. A major portion of this transformation takes place at night. Sleep, particularly deep sleep, allows for contact with the higher vibrations of the underlying field. The result of this contact is to purify the mind and emotions and allow stresses and deep impressions in the mind to be released. Cutting sleep short destroys the stress-releasing process, as the last hours of sleep normal contain much more of the de-stressing time we call dream or REM (rapid eye movement) sleep.

*EXERCISE #1: An Alarm-free Week*

Try going a week without an alarm clock. Get to bed early enough so you awake naturally before the time you would have set on the alarm clock. If you have a significant sleep debt, you may sleep several hours longer than usual, but this will probably only be for a few days. Pay attention to how you feel *after the end of the week*. In particular, what happens to mood and clarity of thinking? (We will have more on sleep in later chapters.)

*EXERCISE #2: Effortless Meditation*

Learn an effortless form of meditation. While concentration techniques may be useful for some people, these are usually best reserved for those cloistered in a monastery. For those in the world, there is quite enough effort, stress, and strain without making the practice of meditation more work. It is easier for the mind to let go and experience the field of bliss with an effortless technique. This is best done with a teacher. Some forms of effortless meditation include Transcendental Meditation, Primordial Sound Meditation and the meditation taught by the Art of Living Foundation.

*EXERCISE #3: Love*

Hardly an exercise, but in that vein, we forget and need to make love a priority. Practice throughout the day for the next week, going inside to that place in your heart where

37

you experience love. Then bring that forth in some expression when the opportunity arises. A "thank you" or an offer of assistance or caring phone call or even just sending kind thoughts from that area of the heart — these all are ways to connect the heart back to love and through that experience back to love's source — the Absolute.


*EXERCISE #4: Asana*
The practice of yoga asana is ultimately to create yoga or "union." In doing so, we unite with the Absolute. While there are many forms of asana practice, those that emphasize spiritual union or the culturing of the heart (such as Anusara Yoga) are often most effective in giving the experience of connecting to the Absolute.

The elements contained in these four exercises are actually important for all aspects of health. Sleep, meditation, love and yoga are powerful nonmaterial tools for the nonmaterial beings that we are. The importance of meditation, however, for the development of awareness cannot be over-emphasized. We cannot be aware of the bliss without expanding our consciousness. In that awareness of inner space we gain the treasures of the kingdom within.

# *3*

## LOVE AND BLISS

In love, bliss finds fulfillment. It finds the flow and the object of adoration to which it can move. Love is so sweet, so natural, so much a part of the fabric of Nature. Creation creates through love. Lovemaking is the underlying theme of the creation. It is its purpose, its method of creating and its goal. In the play of bliss, love finds its goal: the love of God, the love of family, the love of life, the blessed lover.

In Ayurveda the heart is the reservoir of life. It is the container of the eight vital drops of Ojas that make up the connection between worldly and Divine. It is where the soul meets the body and where love resides. In fostering the feelings of bliss, we need only direct the bliss toward a person, and love flows. The contentment that follows makes for a balanced *Sadhaka Pitta*, the physiological seat of the heart's subtle energy.

Ojas is that lively intelligence that mediates between the physical and the nonmaterial, between matter and spirit, and imbues the body with life force. It is the end result of fully metabolizing food, emotion and experience into a pure conductor of consciousness, spirit, *Prana* or life-energy.

Love enhances Ojas because love connects and unites all. It is the flow that unites matter and spirit. Love is the only practical thing in creation, and it is the method by which creation creates. Lost in love, we may not seem practical, but ultimately love is the only practicality because nothing else can nourish us and make us whole at the same time.

## *Love's Reality*

Love is the bliss of the Absolute in motion. It is necessary because it is the source of life flowing to us. It is our nature. Without it, life cannot be sustained because it is the essence of our life force itself. Love is what ultimately sustains us. It is the purity of energy that comes through us and unites us with the organizing power of Nature. It is what sustains human life itself.

Still, we experience this truth so rarely. The emotional heart yearns for this experience of love, and we seek it in so many places... often with such futility. Love is ultimately what makes the human world go 'round. To say that we need love is actually not true. We *are* love. Lost in the illusions of the mind, the details of the practical world, we are as lost to the experience of love, as we are to the experience of the Absolute. Experience love fully — sit in its flow, and allow the flow to settle — and you come to know the Absolute. This is the way of so many devotional paths to the Divine. Difficult they are, as opening to this realm requires such letting go. Letting go of concepts, of the normal sense of self, and more...

Love can be ours through the proper metabolism of emotion. It can be the end product, the result and the by-product of the Ayurvedic way of dealing with emotions.

"Love heals all wounds" because love is the flow of Wholeness through our physiology. There is no greater healer. There is no greater teacher. There is no greater lack in our society at this moment. Nothing is more fundamental to life and to health than love. There is nothing more important to teach. Yet, how many of us were taught about love in school?

Filling the heart with love is the fastest Ayurvedic prescription for Ojas and for health. How do we take this prescription and make it real?

## *Love Heals All*

The Ayurvedic principle is that love heals all. When I was in residency I remember two experienced doctors talking about their experience with geriatrics. They had noted on many occasions that a dying person would hang on in the hospital for days or weeks, awaiting that one last visit from their favorite grandson or granddaughter. Once the long-lost visitor finally made it to the hospital, and the love the elderly person had could finally be expressed, then the life was complete, and the person would pass on. The love they had literally kept them alive until they could see the object of their affection.

This is the power of love. It can sustain us against all odds. It can cure the incurable. It can heal all. Nothing is more important than developing the ability to sustain love in our hearts. It keeps us young. Nothing will make you look younger or keep you from aging as supremely as does love.

Mired in false concepts, we misconstrue love with self-sacrifice. If we truly sacrifice the Self, we crucify love itself. Love comes out of fullness, not emptiness. The sacred books of India called the *Upanishads* say this:

*That is full; this is full. From fullness, fullness comes out.*
*Taking fullness from fullness, what remains is fullness.*

No one teaches us in school about this fullness. No one teaches us how to foster this fullness. No one teaches us how to culture love, to carry love with us, and how to sustain love in our hearts. This is the need of the time. This is the way of Ayurveda and the Yoga of Emotion.

## *The Mental Understanding — Love and Ojas*

Ojas is the finest end product of the process of digestion — all the stages that food goes through in being transformed from one tissue to the next and the next. Processing food into Ojas typically takes about 28 days. While there are some exceptional foods (such as milk) that take a shorter time, generally there is a complex sequential processing necessary to create Ojas. If that processing is blocked by the build-up of toxins (called *Ama*), little Ojas is produced.

Ojas is said to be the mediator between the material and the spiritual. It is the bridge between the physical and the energetic. It is the conduit through which the consciousness is transformed into matter. Ojas is the crowning glory of good digestion and explains why good digestion is so revered in Ayurvedic thinking. Those with good digestion produce more Ojas and have more liveliness, more health and greater longevity.

Classically, Ojas is described as a shiny, white, oily fluid with properties and functions. It is said to:

- Permeate the whole body

- Give strength and immunity

- Give the skin the "glow" of vibrant health

- Be the end product of perfect digestion

- Function as the connection between consciousness and matter

Practically speaking, though, the experience of Ojas is simply the experience of bliss. How does one increase Ojas? How does one experience more bliss?

## *Ways to Increase Ojas*

If you look at most books on Ayurveda, they will contain lists of how to enhance Ojas, often derived from the classical, ancient texts. They include such recommendations as:

- Develop good digestion.

- Eat a balanced diet.

- Develop positivity in feelings, speech, behavior.

- Purify the body/mind through *Panchakarma* or Ayurvedic purification therapies. (These therapies remove impurities from the *Srotas* or channels and are said to improve the cells' ability to wake up and receive Ojas.)

- Take *Rasayanas* or special Ayurvedic herbal preparations that strengthen the body, such as *Amrit Kalash* or *Chyavanprash*.

- Develop consciousness.

- Develop more joy, appreciation and love.

Likewise, they will expound lists of factors that decrease Ojas. The recommendations of things to avoid include such things as:

- Entertaining negative emotions of any kind

- Stress

- Hurrying

- Excessive exercise (Weakness after working out is a sign of reduction of Ojas.)

- Fasting excessively

- Rough or very light diet

- Overexposure to wind and sun

- Staying awake through much of the night

- Excessive loss of body fluids (such as blood)

- Overindulgence in sexual activity

- Injury or trauma to the body

- Alcoholic beverages

A certain difficulty exists in translating from the classical texts. How does one *do* these things? The specifics are often lost. The cart is often put before the horse. Take for example, "developing positivity." The assumption is that one can just pull oneself up by the bootstraps. Except for those rare individuals who have developed a mental habit of seeing everything in positive terms, trying to force oneself to "think positive" doesn't really work. Positivity is the result of a mind that is filled with love and contentment. It is the end result of Ojas, not the starting place. But who can remain in that state all the time?

The recommendations for not "entertaining negativity" must also be explained and understood in a modern context. This does not mean that we never have a negative emotion. Too often people take this phrase to foster more repression of what they have been taught are "negative" emotions. As we shall see, this repression actually causes the negativity to become lodged in the system. The key word in this phrase is "entertaining." To entertain a negative emotion means that we don't let it flow. We create commentary on it. We stimulate it. We give it more time than it is due. We add fuel to the fire, rather than watching it flow and change.

Likewise, the recommendation on sexual activity needs explanation. "Overindulgence" is a personal matter, dependent on body type, age and physical energy. The way one knows if one has overindulged is by changes in mood toward irritability or depression after having sex or the day following sexual activity.

Wakefulness also depletes Ojas. So staying up late or cutting sleep short can interfere in a physical manner with the creation of Ojas. We need to respect and honor the needs of the body so that it can support our metabolizing emotion and transform it to Ojas, bliss and love.

The next chapter will detail ways of developing better emotional digestion. And, of course, keep in mind that eating well is always good for everyone and every condition. Panchakarma (purification therapies) and Rasayanas (rejuvenative herbal formulas) are best done under the direction of an Ayurvedic physician. The last two recommendations under the ways to increase Ojas, however, are the most important. The importance of developing consciousness cannot be overemphasized. That is why it was discussed it in the first chapters of this book.

The final recommendation, though, is also important: Developing love is an equally potent method of creating Ojas. Love incorporates joy, appreciation and acceptance. It is made complex by our associations with religion, family and sexuality, and with the "oughts" and "shoulds" we were taught as children. Too often, out of obligation, we force ourselves to do things in the name of love and suppress any awareness of the feeling level in the process. There is an old Snoopy cartoon where he says, "I love humanity, it's people I can't stand."

The "how to" of the Ayurvedic approach is found in understanding the connection between consciousness and Ojas.

## Consciousness and Ojas

Ojas is like a mini power-relay station. Just as the chakras are major areas for transforming consciousness to energies that are usable by humans, so too is Ojas a transformer on the molecular level. It acts like an antenna and facilitates the reception of consciousness into the body.

The more one meditates and experiences pure consciousness — that area of our existence that is beyond thought, feeling and sensation — the more the body creates Ojas. The body is everso flexible. Whatever we put our attention on creates more connections in our brain and our biochemistry. If we are right-handed and start to play tennis with the left hand, the area of the brain that corresponds to the left hand makes new connections (forms new synapses) and increases the biochemical and neurotransmitter activity in the right parietal lobe (the area that controls movement on the left side of the body). In a like manner, the more one experiences pure consciousness, the more the body produces Ojas. The result is increased energy, liveliness and health.

This is why meditation is so powerful. It not only gives the experience of pure consciousness, it enlivens the body. The refreshed feeling that one experiences after meditating is not simply because one has "taken a break." It is because the whole physical system has been enlivened. This is why "developing consciousness" is listed one of the top two ways of creating Ojas. The other is love.

## *Love and Ojas*

Ojas can be called the "love molecule." It is the physical expression of love as it channels the Divine energy into the physical and allows that part to grow, flourish and ultimately create bliss on the physical level. Feelings of love shower the body with bliss. Being in love creates health. It allows the Divine creative potential to manifest into physical existence. It re-creates the body.

Areas of pain in the body are where the flow of energy is blocked. Bringing the light of love to these areas allows the body to heal. It brings Ojas to the area and provides the bridge from the physical back to the energy and intelligence that enlivens the body. It reconnects back to the template of how the body is intended to be organized. It stimulates the perfect re-creation of the body. In this healing, love has created wholeness, and the byproduct is bliss.

When we cannot metabolize emotional experience — when it is too painful or overwhelming, or when we are taught that certain emotions are unacceptable — then emotional blocks occur. These blocks alter the flow of energy and intelligence to certain areas of the body. They cause constriction and impede our conscious awareness of a particular area of the body. In this environment, Ojas is not created. Metabolism in that area of the body also becomes blocked, and Ojas is no longer produced. This is called emotional Ama or emotional toxicity in the Ayurvedic system. Ama creates disease. It blocks energy and intelligence. It creates complexity. It is the subject of the chapter, "The Drama of Ama."

When we metabolize emotion completely, we come back to self-awareness, back to consciousness, back to the bliss of the Absolute. In that bliss, love flows wherever we direct our attention. That love brings wholeness with it, because it is Wholeness in motion. Ultimately, health is *that* wholeness. This is the power of consciousness. This is the power of the spirit that enlivens the physical. This is why "love heals all." When we metabolize emotion completely, we are free to love. When we don't, love is blocked. The result is pain, either on the level of emotion or, too often, on the level of the body.

The beauty and power of love is that it can also create. It gives energy to create that which is the essence of life. That energy can be directed to creating children or creating art or creating even higher consciousness. The power of love is sufficient to draw two people together from the other side of the world. Through "circumstance" and "happenstance," love will draw together two souls who would never be able to otherwise meet. Love is the ultimate expression of the bliss of existence.

There are no courses on love. Love, like consciousness, is too abstract for far too many of us. Ayurveda makes it concrete, for ultimately Ayurveda is the truth of life, and no clearer truth exists than the fact that love is the center of human life. Ayurveda is full of nurturing and comforting methods to foster love — first of self, then of the Higher Self and ultimately of the world.

The connection between nurturing and fostering love on the level of emotion is undertaken in many different modalities. Massage — touch — is certainly one. Self-massage is clearly part of the daily recommendation and, whenever possible, massage with a trained Ayurvedic technician.

Aromatherapy is another. Scent strikes a cord deep in the brain. It triggers associations and emotional memories that stimulate the awareness and bring balance to emotions. It ultimately nurtures on the emotional level. Often aromas will be recommended to be used at the bedside at night so that the effect on the subconscious mind is even stronger.

Nutrition and cooking are other ways to convey and enhance love. The most important element in Ayurvedic nutrition is the consciousness of the cook. A loving and spiritual cook cannot go wrong in providing for others. The love that is conveyed counters and corrects any imbalance that might occur because of the nature of the food.

The Ayurvedic doctor knows of the research of the Japanese scientist Masaru Emoto who showed that water takes on different crystalline shapes when energetically imbued with love. The patterns of crystals that are formed when it is frozen are beautiful, as compared to those of the energy of hate, war or sadness. The Ayurvedic physician also knows that most of the body is composed of water. In the act of eating, we take in energetically the vibrations of the cook. A loving cook can heal through food.

Love is the end result of perfect emotional digestion. It is the end result of physical digestion. It is a most potent tool in Ayurvedic medicine. Love unites. It brings us out of the illusion of separateness, into the Truth of Life — we are all One.

## The Secret to Love

The secret to love is that it is both the hardest and the simplest thing you will ever do. The consciousness, the life force, travels from the Divine down through the chakras and *we* choose where the flow goes. So love, must first be chosen. This is hard, as the energies for most people naturally travel to the lower three chakras. These first three chakras are intimately connected with the ego. The ego loves to be the focus of the energy. It fears any other choice. This makes love difficult. Why? Because the ego fears love. In love, the ego dissolves, and if there is one overriding purpose behind the ego, it is to survive. In love, there is a merging and a dissolving of the ego. This makes the choosing all so difficult. But once one lets go to this choice, then love is natural and simple and effortless.

The secret to love is more than *just* choosing it. That is the first step. The other step is to become free of the gripping nature of the illusions, memories and emotional impressions that pull the life force away from the sacred heart into the other chakras. These emotions and impressions are the "leftovers" of the inability to fully process experience.

When emotions are fully processed, they leave no residue, and coming back to the Source and to love is ever so easy. The Ayurvedic understanding is that emotion must be fully metabolized or these residues block the natural flow of life, emotion and love. Metabolizing emotion perfectly is the real secret to love.

# *4*

## METABOLIZING EMOTION —
## PERFECTLY

### *The Path*

In being clear, the path is easy to tread. The way of Ayurveda is the way of transformation. We process experience, and it transforms us. We love, and it nourishes us. We feel and we know ourselves. The natural process of feeling and emoting is understood. The process by which feeling becomes bliss and then creates love and consciousness is fully known. Understanding that process and living it is the beauty of this knowledge.

When you are in the murk of emotion, when you are in the "soup" of feeling, the free flow to bliss can be obstructed. The incomplete processing leaves you constipated with intense and often painful feelings that do not flow. Long ago we learned it is not okay to feel or to express and flow with feelings. As children we were "acculturated" into a way of being that did not allow for the emotional life. Much of the feeling life was not acceptable. We were told not to be selfish, not to show anger, not to express our likes, our lusts, our desires. We were taught to be little ladies and gentlemen. In that process, we repressed emotions or were made to feel guilty and ashamed for having them. They became subconscious — something vague and in the background. We were not taught how to be at ease with them, how to experience them, how to allow them to flow and shift and change, nor how to let them be in the awareness without needing to act on them.

When the energy of life expresses itself in emotion and that is blocked, then all life energy can become blocked. Running on half empty, the fullness of life is missed. The bliss remains hidden. Be knowledgeable about the normal processing of emotion. In learning to metabolize emotion, we learn to digest experience. As experience grows, we eventually learn to digest more and more and more, until eventually we learn how to digest the entire universe. We take it and transform it into ourselves. We become the Being that the universe is.

In metabolizing emotion we find a way to bliss. Bliss is the end product of completely digested emotion. Bliss is the nature of the energy behind the motion that is emotion. In the knowledge of Ayurveda, we find treasures that reclaim the lost energy and awareness. Here we find a way to understand and process emotion.

The need is for a way to process emotion... for emotion to be fluid and not binding... for emotion to not leave a residue and get stuck... for the suffering of painful emotions to be released... for emotional blocks to dissolve or never be created... for the body to be allowed to be freed from the impact of the subconscious influence of unreleased emotion... for the emotional body to be freed from the past and thereby free the physical body to heal... for the awareness to allow emotion to flow back to bliss.

## Shankara's Dog

The great Indian sage Shankara was known for his expositions on the nature of the universe and the bliss of existence. He was equally known for seeing only the positive aspects of any situation. Many listeners did not understand his descriptions, and some challenged his sincerity. One day, one of his critics, certain Shankara did not live in this state, decided to prove his descriptions of bliss were just fancy and planned to catch him expressing negativity, exposing him as a fraud. To do this, the critic arranged for the putrid carcass of a dead dog to be placed in the path that Shankara took from his house to the lecture hall where he expounded pure truth. The critic walked with Shankara, and as they came to the dog, the critic exclaimed, "Such a smelling disgusting sight. Why has no one cleaned this up?" He then looked to Shankara. With a smile on his face Shankara said, "A carcass yes, but such pretty white teeth on that dog." The critic was undone. Realizing that Shankara was indeed the enlightened master he was thought to be, the critic threw himself to ground and begged the great Indian sage to be his teacher.

Shankara's enlightened awareness allowed him to metabolize his experience into bliss, positivity and happiness. He spontaneously processed the impressions of the dog into beauty and positivity. This is the way of Ayurveda. This is the understanding of metabolizing emotion and processing it fully. In this way, the end product of digestion is conscious awareness, bliss and happiness.

## The Ayurvedic Understanding: Perfect Metabolism Creates Perfect Emotional Freedom

Metabolism means to convert energy from one form to another. In the human body, metabolism is the transformation of food into physical energy — the energy needed for maintaining body temperature, for circulating blood and for moving the musculature. The process by which the conversion takes place is understood in detail in Ayurveda. It is called *Agni*. Literally translated, Agni means "fire." Digestion is viewed as a fire in Ayurveda, and when the fire burns brightly any wood thrown on it transforms completely into energy. Ayurveda understands that there is a sequential stepwise processing that is required for complete digestion. At each stage another Agni is present.

Just as medical science recognizes fundamental body tissues, so too does Ayurveda. Seven tissue layers are described, each one nourishing the next. If the Agni responsible for the transformation is burning brightly. The seven *Dhatus* or tissue layers are:

- *Rasa* or blood plasma or the fluid the blood cells are bathed in
- *Rakta* or the blood cells
- *Mamsa* or muscle tissue
- *Meda* or fat tissue
- *Asthi* or bone tissue
- *Majja* or bone marrow
- *Shukra* or reproductive tissues or fluids

Each tissue level nourishes the next level. Rasa supplies the nutrients that bathe and nourish the blood cells (Rakta). The red blood cells carry oxygen to the muscles (Mamsa). When we stop working out, muscle "turns to fat" as the muscle tissue is "transformed" to fat tissue. In stepwise fashion, each level nourishes the next. At each level a specialized form of Agni is responsible for transforming one tissue substance or energy into something the next tissue layer needs in order to be healthy. Obviously, if the Agni at one level is not burning properly, it will cause the next tissue layer to be malnourished.

Emotional digestion parallels physical digestion. Emotional digestion also has a specific sequence, and a weak Agni at any level creates problems for the frictionless flow of feeling to return back to its source.

Physical digestion takes place in a methodical manner, just like assembling a car on an assembly line. At the beginning, a car is just an empty chassis. As it moves down the line, parts are added in a logical and predetermined manner. Likewise with physical digestion. Digestion begins in the mouth, both in terms of the chewing process and in terms of digestive enzymes. Enzymes such as amylase start breaking down starches and other aspects of the food in the mouth. After chewing, the bolus of food travels to the next station on the line, the stomach. Here a different set of enzymes and acids continue the transformative process. These are called *Jathar-Agni* in Ayurvedic terminology. Food then travels to the small intestine where further processing occurs and some of the elements of the food are transported from the small intestine to the first tissue layer (Rasa). This then starts the transformation process that nourishes all the tissues of the body.

Imagine what can happen here if the sequencing or the processing is not correct. Say we ingest too much. It's like when the worker on the line, who is ready to put a car seat on the chassis, is suddenly confronted with a dilemma: Two chassis appear. There is not enough time to put chairs in both, so one car ends up defective or "malformed."

Imagine also what happens if the power tools that the line worker is using are underpowered. The screws to hold the seat onto the chassis may not be tight enough to hold. The seat becomes wobbly, loose, and moves to interfere with the placement of the transmission that goes between the two front seats. The "power tool" of physical digestion is Agni. (Think *strong* digestive enzymes if you need a physical concept.) The power tool of emotional digestion is awareness.

The entire digestive system is designed to re-create physical experience. The end process of digestion, the end product, after all seven tissue layers have been nourished, is called Ojas in Ayurveda. It is still in the physical realm, perhaps akin to a potent hormone or neurotransmitter, but it conveys almost pure liveliness to the body. It is perceived on the body as a glowing face, a lively attitude or as vibrant health. It is the conduit through which energy comes into the physical from the higher vibrations of consciousness.

Just as the entire physical experience is designed to re-create physical existence, the entire emotional system is designed to re-create the feeling experience. The end process of emotion is love or the emotional expression of unity and divinity — bliss.

The process by which we experience and metabolize emotion is similar to that which takes place on the physical level with digestion and metabolism:

- First, we must ingest, not block.
- Second, we must taste, not rush past.

- Third, we must swallow, not reject.

- Fourth, we must transform, not be overwhelmed.

- Fifth, we must absorb and integrate, not follow old patterns where emotions got stuck.

- Sixth, we must eliminate, not hang on.

- Seventh, we must create Ojas, return to Self, and create love and bliss.

When we don't process emotion fully, it sticks to us like slimy, old sputum on a counter. It gets lodged in our emotional body and hampers flow, particularly in the chakras and the substations called *Marmas* that they most directly feed.

## Integration — Emotional Processing and the Dhatus

Of all the steps in the process of digestion, absorption and integration are most important. For emotional experience to nourish us and create energy, love and bliss, this stage of emotional processing must be complete. This parallels the processing that takes place on the level of the Dhatus. For each physical expression there is an emotional counterpart. The process of absorbing, transforming and integrating the "good" elements — the useful elements — and eliminating those that are not useful is the focus of the Agnis that work between each Dhatu. Each Dhatu carries its emotional counterpart.


### *Rasa or Blood Plasma — Keyword: Nourish*

Rasa is the clear, plasma portion of your blood that carries nutrients absorbed from your intestines to your entire body. There is a special connection between Rasa and the skin and mucous membranes. When out of balance, the skin is dull, the entire body is malnourished and there are often sores or dryness of the mucous membranes.

Rasa is most easily disturbed by factors that affect the overall strength of your digestion. Fasting, eating meals at irregular times, not drinking enough water, eating a lot of dry foods (chips, crackers, popcorn, dry cereals), consuming too much salt, skipping or delaying meals (especially when you're hungry), eating when you're *not* hungry or before your previous meal is fully digested, overeating — these all can throw off the first state of absorption and integration. Rasa can also be disturbed by staying up late at night and not getting enough sleep. Resisting experience, which often manifests as breathing shallowly and holding your breath when stressed, is a key factor in disturbing Rasa. Stress, worry and fear all create resistance and block absorption and integration on the Rasa level.

The emotional counterpart is clear. Rasa bathes and nourishes the lifeblood. Resisting emotional experience or attempting to engage in another intense emotional experience *before* the last experience was processed leads to an imbalance in Rasa. Such an imbalance fundamentally cuts off *all* absorption and integration.

Physically, the challenge for Rasa imbalance is disturbance in the whole digestion process. Emotionally, the challenge is one of awareness of emotion. Out of fear we repress emotion and push it out of our awareness. The challenge is fear versus love. Love accepts all, embraces all, is all-compassionate and forgiving. It forgives and gives over to the Higher Order of the Universe all evaluation and assessment. In love, it accepts whatever comes, as it comes. It embraces each emotion and allows it to be tasted without fear or evaluation.

Having been acculturated into an illusion of acceptable and unacceptable emotions, we hamper emotional digestion by cutting off what we judge as something we should not be feeling. This stops emotional nurturance at its root and stops digestion before it even gets started.

To rebalance Rasa physically, we "drink in" life. We rehydrate the body with water, juicy fruits and vegetables. These help to build up and nourish the clear part of the blood, as well as purifying it. On a physical level, Rasa symptoms can be resolved by eating one or two sweet juicy fruits every day and drinking plenty of pure, room-temperature water. Doing these things with the intention of self-nurturance can aid Rasa digestion on the emotional level.

On that level, the message is clear: Drink in emotional experience, be fully present, sit in the emotion and feel where it is experienced in the physical. Let yourself be aware of emotion without judgment. Nurture the feeling level. Slow down, so that emotional digestion can take place. Relax more. Get more sleep, so that you can be clearer about what is flowing through your emotional sphere at each moment during the day. Finally, give yourself an *Abhyanga* (self oil massage) each day. (See instructions at the end of the book.)

## *Rakta or Red Blood Cells — Keyword: Flow*

Rakta refers to the red blood cells and bile, which is composed largely of the breakdown products of red blood cells. Rakta is most easily disturbed by the types of foods you eat and your emotional life. Very acidic foods (tomatoes, fermented foods), very alkaline foods (leavened with baking soda), and toxins (alcohol, nicotine, drugs, chemicals) aggravate Rakta, as does continual frustration or anger. Whereas Rasa represents nourishment, Rakta represents that which carries oxygen, and its energetic aspect called *Prana*, to the rest of the body. Red blood cells carry oxygen and nourish and feed the entire body. There is a sense of dynamism here, of movement or flow that creates problems (heat or friction) when obstructed. Rakta, even when it is not obstructed, is prone to become "hot" due to its energetic nature. That is why hot emotions (anger, frustration, passion) can create a physical imbalance in this tissue layer. On a physical level, if your Rakta is disturbed, avoid hot, spicy or very salty foods or very acidic foods like vinegar.

Also avoid alcoholic beverages, recreational drugs (including marijuana), fermented foods (including sourdough breads and soy sauce), and aged cheeses (including Parmesan and feta). These are all heating to the blood. Avoid fasting, as well. When fasting, the body's Agni has nothing to burn, so it starts to literally burn the body instead, and this can cause the blood to heat up. Symptoms associated with hot blood include rashes, acne, eczema, psoriasis, gallbladder problems, heavy menstrual periods and awakening in the middle of the night.

Emotionally, to help maintain your bliss, avoid violence, watching violent movies or news shows, and going to bed late (after 10 P.M.). More fundamentally, in processing emotions be conscious of the need for control and the need for life to go as exactly as you want it.

Rakta's "seat" or "origin" is said to be in the gallbladder and liver. Even Chinese medicine acknowledges that the liver provides a flowing and spreading function. When the *chi* of the liver gets stuck or stagnant it can create frustration and depression. Underlying this is often issues of control.

For Ratka's flow to be unhindered, the flow of emotion must remain unhindered. Control is opposed to flow and often hides fear or profound attachment, whether to possession, concept or plan. Control destroys the processing of emotion. Because we were never taught how to *manifest* our desires, we become attached to trying to control life and its outcomes. Obviously, we can never control everything, so this is a paradoxical exercise in futility. Futility is the breeding ground for frustration, and frustration of desire is the primary cause of Rakta imbalance from the emotional perspective.

When we don't attempt to control emotion and our experience of it, we notice this: The longer we observe an emotion, how it feels, where we feel it in the body, how intense it is, etc., the more the emotion changes. At first, it may just decrease in intensity. But then the quality will change, and it may even flow into another emotion. Emotions contain "motion." They move and flow. When we intervene and "stick" the emotion in place, then the possibility of Rakta imbalance is created.

To purify and balance Rakta on the physical level, we follow a diet of more neutral tastes (not excessively spicy, sour or salty) with plenty of pure water and organic fruits and vegetables.

On an emotional level, cultivating a more forgiving and tolerant state of mind through meditation is extremely useful. Also, working with the process of attending to emotions (Rasa level) and allowing them to flow naturally (Rakta level) can be akin to a spiritual practice. Letting go and letting the Divine work out the details is the key, for the control is never really possible. The desires are fulfilled through the workings of Nature. In letting go and trusting, we allow the flow that will ultimately flow into the field of bliss.

## *Mamsa or Muscles — Keyword: Consolidation*

Mamsa refers to the muscle tissue in your body, which includes the uterus, blood vessels, glands, bladder, bowels and heart. Muscle tissue is formed through consolidating all that is carried from the blood (Rasa and Rakta). Mamsa is the physical representation of the consolidation and integration of the essence derived from food. In consolidating on the emotional level, the awareness becomes heightened to the essence of the emotion, and we begin to integrate or intuit its meaning. When Mamsa is out of balance there is too much consolidation. A sticky, slimy substance called *Ama* is formed that can get deposited in the body, interfering with proper tissue formation. Ama will block the flow of energy in the body. It results in soreness, fatigue, sleepiness after eating a big meal, weight gain and ultimately in diseases like atherosclerosis (hardening of the arteries). On an emotional level, when Mamsa is out of balance there is a tendency to hang onto emotional experience. Rather than stopping the flow, as in a Rakta imbalance, with Mamsa out of alignment, the emotion tends to get replayed and restimulated and eventually imbedded and stuck in the subconscious mind and in the cells of the body.

On a physical level, Mamsa is most easily disturbed by factors that promote the formation of dense, sticky and clogging Ama from foods. This includes foods that are old, leftover, and foods that are cold, dense, rich or heavy (such as cheeses, deli foods and ice cream). Leftover or impure or nonorganic meat is especially disturbing to your body's muscle tissue. Since these foods are made of muscle themselves, they tend to affect your body's muscles directly, providing either good protein nourishment or toxic substances to your muscles.

On an emotional level, the tendency to analyze emotion and create scenarios or stories around it often only serves to stick the feeling into the subconscious mind. Replaying the stimulus for the emotion, or repeating the words we create around the feelings, only serves to create emotional Ama. Say someone cuts in front of us in line, and we feel some anger and tell ourselves, "This is not right." If we continue to repeat this phrase and weave more story around the injustice — say we begin a commentary about how people are less respectful than they used to be and how society is falling apart, or we reflect on how unfair other things in our life have been — then we get stuck in the feeling, and emotional Ama or toxicity is the result.

To balance and purify Mamsa on a physical level, pursue activities that tone and strengthen your muscles and increase circulation to them, such as yoga, stretching, exercise and a daily oil massage. Also, follow a lighter, preferably vegetarian diet. Eat one or two dates per day and one cup cooked buckwheat at least once a week. Strictly avoid red meat, pork and cheese.

On an emotional level, observing emotion and allowing its meaning to come to you intuitively is more useful than analysis. This occurs later in the processing. At the Mamsa stage, it would be better not to interpret the emotion at all lest we risk creating emotional Ama. With the person who cuts in line, we observe the anger and feel perhaps some injustice, but then we allow the emotion to flow and change. In this process, you will notice for a bit that the attention you give the emotion *intensifies* its experience. It causes a consolidation of the experience, even as the emotions flows and changes. You become aware of all the *flavors* of anger, just as you will come to know all the flavors of joy, as you learn to consolidate that emotion.

*Meda or Fat and Hormones — Keyword: Facilitate*

Meda refers to the fat tissue, hormones and carbohydrate metabolism. When it is out of balance, we gain weight by looking at food. We have hormonal imbalances that disturb the natural rhythms of the body. When in balance, hormones facilitate the transformation of substance into energy and are responsible for regulating metabolism in general.

This level of processing facilitates the transformation of emotion back into energy stores, redirected back into the underlying field, the Absolute.

Physically Meda is most easily disturbed by factors that clog up and slow down metabolism, such as eating too much fat or sugar, not exercising enough, eating too many calories and eating too much in the evening.

If Meda is physically disturbed, avoid eating refined carbo-hydrates (sweets, cookies, cakes, chips, crackers, etc.), French fries or any other deep-fried foods, curdled foods (cheese, yogurt) in the evening, and heavy foods like meat or cheese or creamy, rich foods on a regular basis. Avoid cooking with impure oils such as nonorganic, refined vege-table oils, lard or genetically modified canola oil, Eating late at night (after 8 P.M.) and consuming excess fat also dis-turbs Meda. To resolve Meda symptoms, get more exercise. The following foods are especially good for Meda imbal-ance: bran; whole cooked grains (especially barley and quinoa); green, leafy vegetables (chard, kale, spinach and broccoli) and legumes (lentils, dahl, dried beans and peas).

From the emotional perspective, we can facilitate the trans-formation of emotion back into energy by allowing the awareness to experience the part of the body that gets ener-gized by the emotion. Where do we feel it? What aspect of the physical gets enhanced and enlivened? In what way do we feel to move to release the bond between the memory and the energy it carries? Converting the energy of emotion into physical motion allows the memory to be detoxified. We no longer have to experience the emotion again and again when the energy has been released. The memory can come without impact.

## *Asthi or Bone — Keyword: Support*

Asthi refers to bone tissue and what Ayurveda calls its metabolic "relatives" — cartilage, hair, teeth and nails — where symptoms of poor Asthi nourishment may appear and cause diseases such as osteoarthritis. Just as bone is our supporting tissue, emotional support strengthens us as well.

Asthi is most easily disturbed by factors that aggravate the nervous system, such as late nights, mental stress and irregular meals. It is no coincidence that major depression increases the risk of osteoporosis.

Physically, to keep bones strong, you need adequate dietary calcium and vitamin D. However, you also need good digestion and assimilation to allow these nutrients to be absorbed.

Emotionally, we need to create the structure to support the emotional processing. This means honoring our emotions, trusting them, respecting them and creating *the time* to retrain how we process them. Often this means some alone time, and definitely the process of meditation can help here. Support your emotional processing, and your emotions will support you. Give them space and time, and rather than having to look outside yourself for emotional support, you will find that the fulfillment they can bring will support you. The self-nurturance of a walk in the rising sun or the daily oil massage can emotionally strengthen your support system. They allow you to create space to feel, while simultaneously strengthening your bones.

## *Majja or Bone Marrow — Keyword: Integrity*

Majja includes not only bone marrow, the main production site for blood cells and immune cells, but also the immune system and brain.

Imbalance in Majja can mean that the immune system is not functioning optimally. "Adrenal exhaustion," inability to handle stress and chronic lack of stamina are common symptoms of Majja weakness. When you are exhausted there is no way to integrate emotional experience into a stronger sense of personal integrity. In this state, you become overly susceptible to other people's energies.

When the body has a Majja imbalance, it is very important to get more rest, do gentle but regular exercise, give yourself a daily oil massage, and eat very healthy and pure, wholesome foods to help restore the strength to the immune system and strengthen the resilience of your nervous system. To resolve Majja symptoms, avoid junk food and processed foods, and eat organic foods as much as possible. Eat warm, oily, nurturing foods like milk, walnuts, pecans, blanched almonds, mangoes and ghee (clarified butter).

From an emotional perspective, sleep is the key to restoring energy, wholeness and integrity. In the processing of emotions, integrity comes from allowing the emotional experience to affirm oneself and one's wisdom.

In the cutting-in-line example, we first come to an awareness of the feeling of injustice or anger (Rasa). We notice how this flows (Rakta) and shifts. We experience its intensification and consolidation (Mamsa). We notice how it facilitates more energy flow to the body, particularly in the center of the torso (Meda), and we notice how this energy supports our liveliness (Asthi). As we complete the processing of the emotion, it may come to us that this situation has been created for us to learn patience. We want others to have patience with our faults, so we will choose to have patience with theirs. As we integrate the emotional experience, we allow its purpose and perfection to bolster our integrity, our purpose and our strength. Standing in our wisdom, we become stronger, more self-sufficient and less readily swayed by outside influence. We are then ready for the final step in the emotional integration process.

*Shukra or Reproductive Essence — Keyword: Create*

Shukra relates to the reproductive essence of the body: the ovum or eggs in females, the sperm in males, the reproductive fluids, and the reproductive system in general. Shukra is also closely related to immune function and overall strength and stamina. If it is well-nourished and maintained and not unduly spent on sexual functions, then it supports the production of Ojas, the life-giving essence of the body that also protects it from outside influence and gives it strength and immunity.

Physically, Shukra is most easily disturbed by factors that deplete energy, immune system strength and nutrition, or those that overtax the reproductive system, such as too much sexual activity or too frequent childbirth (babies less than two years apart). Emotionally, Shukra is depleted when we overwhelm ourselves with attempting to process much more than we can handle or force ourselves to be creative when we are emotionally drained.

To balance Shukra on the physical level, moderation in all your habits, including sexual activity, is useful. Get enough sleep (at least eight hours), go to bed by 10 P.M., and give yourself a daily oil massage. Eat nurturing foods like milk, fresh asparagus, walnuts, pecans, blanched almonds and mangoes when they are in season, and eat one sweet, juicy pear or apple each day.

Emotionally, once we have completed the integration process (Majja), we are ready to let go of any residual energy and come back to the bliss of the Self. We allow our attention to come to our hearts and experience the love that resides there, and then let that flow into silence and experience the bliss of the Absolute once again. In this silence, in this bliss we are Creators. Anything we intend, anything we put our attention on in that silence, starts the whole ocean to move directing Nature to create the fulfillment of our desire. In letting go and coming back to silence, back to bliss, we become completely liberated from the past, from the influence of the emotional experience, and we stand free in our ability to create whatever we want. The result of this creative process is the emotional experience of bliss. The physical expression of this bliss is the creation of a new life and the joy and excitement felt when a couple, desiring a child, learn that their desire will be fulfilled.

## *Designed for Bliss*

A loud noise startles us, and we laugh, "Wow, that woke me up." The noise creates a moment of fear. The experience of fear is to wake us up to the illusion of separateness, of mortality, and for us to see through that illusion and come back to the feeling of wholeness and the immortality of the present moment. In that process we re-create ourselves more awake and more aware and more in divine love.

Anger creates the illusion of self power and when fully processed establishes us in Divine Power, the bliss of the self.

Guilt creates the illusion of righteousness — and establishes us in the Divine Path.

Depression creates the illusion of limited possibilities — and establishes within us our ability to let go and let God.

Insecurity creates the illusion of worth — and establishes us in the infinite worth of the Divine and the infinite love of the Divine.

Desire creates the illusion of external happiness — and establishes in us the infinite happiness of the Divine.

All emotion is a correction, a rebalancing that leads us back to love and back to the Higher Self, back to the Divine. All emotion is a fluctuation in the field, a disturbance in the even pond of bliss that creates movement. If that movement is allowed to flow naturally, then it leads back to the Source and back to love, back to Divinity.

When we identify with emotion and wrap ourselves in it and feel we *are* it, we give into our conditioning and cause ourselves to dwell in the emotion and interpret and reinterpret it in terms of our past experience. This creates further involvement. However, when we learn to metabolize emotion perfectly, we just observe the rise and fall of emotion. That is all that is necessary. Each emotion flows to more awareness, to more wisdom, and back to the infinite bliss within.

## Homework: Practicing the Process

Perfect metabolism of emotion does not take place overnight. It requires practice. Know the steps and practice the process:

- Attend to the feeling.

- Observe how it flows and changes.

- Observe how it consolidates and intensifies.

- Observe what part of the body it energizes — allow it to facilitate more liveliness in the body and allow the body to move with it.

- Give time to support your observation and nurture yourself so that the practice *supports you.*

- Intuit the purpose and meaning of the emotional experience *without analysis.*

- Let go of the experience and return to silence, ready to create a new experience or implement the wisdom you have gained.

*5*

# THE DRAMA OF AMA

## *Ama*

Understand that in the play of creation we have free will that allows us to stick things to the pure Being, the pure consciousness that we are. We are beings of light and that light is shown through a myriad of prisms and filters. In the emotional sphere, when the normal ebb and flow of feeling is halted, then emotional Ama is the result.

Ama is the concept in Ayurveda of "toxin." Most toxins are thought to occur not from the environment but from our inability to fully process and break down food, experience and emotion. The sticky, gooey residue blocks the proper flow of energy and intelligence from the depths of the Unified Field to the conscious mind and the physical body.

In having free will, we can choose to hold on to thoughts and emotions. We can choose food and experience that is not in tune with our nature. And we can choose to process things in a manner that make for maldigestion. This concept of free will is embodied in what is described as the root cause of disease in Ayurveda: *Pragya Aparad.* This is translated as "violation of nature" or "mistake of the intellect." Because we can halt emotion and feeling and ignore it, push it out of awareness or stop its flow by creating thoughts, images and stories about it that stick the emotion to our experience, we can create Ama. We can violate the natural flow of emotion and feeling. We can halt the processing and digesting of experience. Free will allows us to choose to engage in overwhelming experiences, overstimulation of the senses, bombardment of the mind. When we do more than our individual nature can handle, then we have "violated nature." But most importantly we can choose to do what is in tune with our innermost selves. We can love and accept our nature. We can choose to feel the wonderful peace that comes in accepting each emotion as it flows forth.

In this peace, in this acceptance we establish our awareness in the depths of the silence of the Absolute. We establish our "intellect" in that being and effortlessly express our nature. The "intellect" in Vedic terms is simply the mind's ability to discriminate and decide between this and that. In this free will we can decide to do things against our nature. In the process of developing consciousness, our awareness becomes more aligned with the depths of the Absolute and our decisions are spontaneously aligned with Nature. We choose what almighty Nature wants for us. We establish ourselves in the bliss of the lap of Nature. All is provided. All is taken care of. We establish ourselves in the trusting hand of Nature. We root ourselves in the love of Nature. We become one with Nature and express the intelligence of being in harmony with every aspect.

In this bliss we are beyond disease. When we fall away from this or are never told that it exists and that we can grow into it, then suffering results. We engross ourselves in the thoughts that stick the emotions to us. Someone cuts us off on the road, and anger flares as we lean on the car horn. But then the mind steps in. We justify our anger and talk to ourselves about how inconsiderate people are, about why they are not more careful, about how dangerous driving is, about what should be done to such people, and on and on and on. The surge of biochemicals in the body that accompanies our anger strikes at our tissues and eats at them. In stimulating anger we always receive the first blow, regardless of the fight. Our bodies are hit with a surge of stress hormones, and the damage is done before we can shake a fist or bring the voice to yell.

The drama of Ama is in this: We create a story around the emotion that reverberates in the subconscious mind with the old interpretations of experience, the old storylines we created. It is story because no interpretation can ever be the full truth of the old experience. It is just a representation of some aspect of it.

We stand to give a speech and the nerves run wild. The heart races. "What will people think?" The voice falters, the applause is muted, and we assume we have failed. The subconscious memory of school is activated, and we recall receiving a low grade or having our answer in class criticized. We feel stupid, ashamed. The story around one of our parents criticizing us is activated. We relate to the feeling level of being told we are inadequate, and we tell ourselves this story again, reinforcing it and further lodging the Ama in our psyche. The "real story" is much fuller and may actually run something like this:

*We are to give the speech. The eyes of almost everyone in the first three-quarters of the audience turn to us for the guidance and the inspiration they will receive. They are open to hearing, but more importantly to feeling and experiencing what we have to say. Their attentiveness in and of itself is speaking volumes in terms of respect and admiration. We are so wrapped up in ourselves that we do not feel, see or appreciate this. We do not sense the energy of anticipation and the respect being offered in the room. We focus on the one-quarter of the audience in the back four rows who does not seem to be attentive. While they are looking to the podium occasionally, they are whispering among themselves. We see this as exchanging criticism about the content of the talk we are presenting. What we don't see is what is actually happening there:*

*Ms. Windmere got a phone call just prior to the start of the talk informing her that her grandmother was just rushed to the hospital. She is talking to her friend, wondering if she should call her sister and have her go to the hospital to meet their mother.*

*Mr. Philips is having trouble with his marriage and has been having difficulty concentrating at work. He is worried about losing his job and is wondering how to keep his thoughts from racing and his anxiety from showing. He is wondering if he will start breaking out in a sweat again from the panic.*

*Mrs. Bloomfield is severely depressed. She is sitting in the back because she showed up late. She has just started on her third antidepressant and is so spaced out she loses track of time. She has difficulty following conversations because she is overmedicated, but she doesn't know it. To compensate she leans over ask the person next to her what you just said. The person she asks is slightly irritated and frowns a little as she leans over to explain. You take the frown to mean that she is irritated by what you just said in the speech.*

And so it goes. The Ama of old patterning distracts you from perceiving what is really going on. It prevents you from sensing the overall energy of the room and recognizing the vast majority of people are showing interest, even enthusiasm in your presentation.

The two key causative patterns of suffering, from the Ayurvedic perspective, are emotional Ama and imbalance (of the Doshas). While the later requires a more detailed explanation, it is usually Ama that prevents the natural rebalancing processes from occurring. Ama is the main culprit in most emotional suffering.

The task before us is to animate that which will serve us and those around us. The light of consciousness animates whatever it illuminates. In knowing this, we take on the task of eliminating emotional Ama so that we may be free and innocent in each moment.

"Letting go" is the mental act of attempting to release the old patterning. The patterning of emotional Ama creates alterations within the nervous system itself that must be addressed. It is as if memory were integrated into the cellular structure of the body. Letting go of the past requires a new approach. The old psychology no longer serves, as it takes great time and expense, as well as great skill and expertise on the part of the therapist. But something more is needed. The Ayurvedic sages understood this. They knew that releasing does not take place simply as an act of will or as the result of a decision. They knew that this release could only occur when all the various frequencies of consciousness through which the human operates are purified of the old patterning.

Purification therapy in Ayurveda is thought to be one of the most important aspects of maintaining health. It is considered a specialty in Ayurveda, just as cardiology or rheumatology is in allopathic or Western medicine. Purification must take place on all levels of vibration — the physical, or body patterning of physical movement and posture that holds the associated "memory" of the emotion, as well as the physical by-products of the neurohormonal stimulation that embed themselves into the tissues in various areas of the body. The "energetic" memory is held in the etheric body, and this must be released also. On the astral or emotional plane of existence, the emotional exists as a substance that has a taste, odor, texture, look and feel that can lodge in the aura and requires a letting go and releasing process in order to purify. On the mental level, the thoughts and story created around the feeling must be dismantled and released. On the causal level, the subconscious patterning that creates the tendency for the repetition of the emotional situation must be released. Finally, on the spiritual level, the overtones of the emotion and the tendency for the consciousness to identify with the emotions must be purified out of the system.

On each level, the process of releasing emotional Ama and imbalance requires purification. The system of Panchakarma involves elements that address each of the levels of consciousness, each of the vibrations of consciousness.

The drama of emotional Ama can get quite complex. In fact, the hundreds of approaches to psychology and self-help attest to its complexity. But the ancients knew a few secrets about these matters. They knew the interaction of the mind and the body, of the physical structure and the energetic anatomy. They also knew ways to effectively free the body of Ama *on all levels.* This Panchakarma therapy is an integral part of becoming free of the emotional Ama that creates suffering in life.

## *Heart to Heart — Compassion*

When we realize the play that Ama creates in us, we understand the struggle others undergo. We see how they suffer, stuck in the repetitive patterns of old emotions, old hurts and fears. In order to keep from re-experiencing the pain of these emotions, we create resistance. We block conscious awareness from attending to the experience and therefore do not process or metabolize it. We do not transform its energies into something useful, do not promote the energy of the emotion into a higher level of bliss. We have no model for doing this, no teacher or training for how this takes place. Instead we stick the memory to our psyche and to our physical being.

When we realize that criticism coming from the person next to us is a result of emotional Ama, our perception and reaction changes. Someone complains that they find us "too pushy," and the typical reaction is to feel taken aback. With the knowledge of emotional Ama, we can see deeper into the situation. We can see that this person offering the complaint was taken advantage of by her siblings and has great fear that others will not respect her. We understand that she is relating to her fears of being taken advantage of and her need to feel better about herself and that her criticism most likely has absolutely nothing to do with us. She is not relating to us *at all*. She is relating to her emotional Ama, created from years of patterning during her childhood. Once this is realized we don't take the criticism to heart. It is not "personal." We don't have to own it as a comment on us, because it is not — it is a comment on her relating to the past. With this realization we can perceive deeper into her emotional space and understand how difficult her life must be — carrying this baggage from the past, afraid to assert herself (because then she will be "like them"), avoiding the most competent people, those who actually have the most to teach her. We then understand her fear and the incredible bind this emotional Ama creates for her, and then we can have only one reaction — compassion.

Understanding emotional Ama and how it motivates behavior can only lead to compassion. We understand. We are able to not be taken in by the fear, the anger, the hurt or the criticism. It does not mean that we become a doormat and allow others to abuse us. When we understand the source of an attack as coming only from old Ama, we spare ourselves the pain and create many alternate reactions.

With this knowledge we understand that all competitiveness, all criticism and "put-downs," are reactions to feelings of unworthiness, insecurity, and low self-esteem. All anger is a reaction to hurt or fear. All rejection is a reaction to fear of intimacy. All lack of caring is a reaction to being stuck in the illusion of isolation. All fear is a reaction to the illusion of separateness. All hurt is a reaction to attachment.

Once understanding ensues, compassion follows. This is the beauty of understanding emotional Ama.

## How It Works

Once emotional energy is stimulated it flows through the subtle energy system to the physical. At this point several options present themselves. Either the energy dissipates, gets transformed to a higher vibration or to a lower vibration, or it gets resisted and stuck. Once stuck it alters posture, movement, mental and emotional reactions and can even get embedded into the cellular make-up via the neurotransmitters that influence the composition of the neurotransmitter receptors in the cell.

What we attend to grows. If we attend to the pain, we hold onto it. If we attend to how it changes, it changes. If we attend to how we can transform it, it transforms. If we attend to resisting it, we get stuckness. The energy stagnates and stays put. An energy drain is created whereby we must put energy forth to resist the emotional experience from coming back to awareness.

Mental processes will reinforce the resistance to change. We develop a belief around the emotional experience that then influences not only our behavior but also encases and crystallizes the emotional Ama that has energetically embedded itself in our physiology.

Consciousness is like a culture medium that is used to grow bacteria. It is sticky. It is nourishing. Things grow if they stay there long enough.

*The drama of Ama is the incredible complexity of energies and emotions that weave the inner dialogue and experience and create the story we tell ourselves about our lives, the people in them, and the events that happen to us. Life is dramatic, and drama is not all bad. It engages us in life. It keeps us interested and motivated. But it is to be enjoyed. It is to be enjoyed and to create joy. It is the drama of how the good will get the better of the bad, how it will all turn out, how the seriousness will fall away to the laughter and bliss of human existence. It is when the energy gets stuck and we cannot escape the pain of the drama that we suffer. Clearing the Ama brings back the joy and the bliss. It allows us to just be. Just be in bliss. Just be in love.*

## *6*

# THE DANCE OF THE DOSHAS

## *The Dance*

Out of the field arises creation. Each aspect of creation takes on certain qualities and leaves behind others. It cannot include all the potential qualities contained in the underlying field of all potentiality. It is that which we call *Dosha* that the ancients used to describe the quality that rises up. It means impurity. Is all of creation impure? Only in the sense that it cannot contain the entire field. All of creation arises first as a vibration of potentiality. These are the fundamental vibratory elements. They are given the names of earth, water, fire, air and space, but they are not these "things." They are the qualities or vibrations carried by such substances. Air-like substances have more of the "air" quality or *Mahabhuta*. The Mahabhutas combine into more gross vibrations to form the Doshas. Doshas are still in the virtual or unmanifest state and guide creation. They serve as the design template for creation.

The three Doshas are *Vata, Pitta and Kapha.* Vata is composed of air and space and is responsible for all things light and airy. Like the wind, it moves things in a subtle manner. It is responsible for flow and dispersion, for respiration and the movement of electrical impulses in the nervous system in the human body. Vata is responsible for mental clarity and for enthusiasm and excitement, liveliness and vibrancy. And when out of balance, like a cold wind that makes us shiver, it causes us to shake with nervousness, anxiety and fear.

Pitta is composed of fire with a little moisture (water). Pitta represents the transforming process in Nature. It is responsible for digestion and metabolism. It brings warmth and heat and the ability to break things down, to analyze on the level of the mind. It is responsible for passion and desire, for motivation and organization. It brings light and heat wherever it goes.

Kapha is composed of earth and water. It creates the heavy solidness of creation. It is the structure that gives strength and endurance. It is responsible for lubrication and immunity in the human physiology. It gives heaviness and steadiness. It brings joy and an easy-going quality to the personality.

The details of the qualities of the Doshas and how they can be applied to various aspects of creation are listed below:

## *VATA*

- Fundamental Elements: space and air
- Qualities: light, dry, coarse, rough, dark, changeable, moveable, subtle, etc.
- Body- type: light build, thin
- Handshake: cold, thin, weak
- Psychology: enthusiastic, vivacious, talkative
- Foods: cold, raw, rough (salads), dry (beans), light (popcorn)
- Colors: dark-blue, black, dark-brown
- Season: fall, early winter
- Time of day: 2-6 A.M. or P.M.
- Location in Physiology: colon, joints, inside of bones
- Function in Physiology: movement, transportation, communication (nervous system moves information, so is ruled by Vata)

## *PITTA*

- Fundamental Elements: fire (plus a little moisture)
- Qualities: hot, sharp, pungent, intense, flowing (but grounded)
- Body-type: medium build, muscular
- Handshake: crushing grip, warm hand
- Psychology: intense, analytical, focused, generous, goal-oriented

- Foods: hot, spicy (chilies, ginger), burning or acidic (vinegar, citrus)
- Colors: orange, light intense-blue
- Season: summer
- Time of day: 10-2 A.M. or P.M.
- Location in Physiology: liver, small intestine, skin
- Function in Physiology: digestion and metabolism

## KAPHA

- Fundamental Elements: earth and water
- Qualities: unctuous (oily), slimy, cool, moist, sticky, heavy, stable, strong, soft
- Body-type: large build
- Handshake: soft puffy pillow
- Psychology: jovial, sweet, loving, easy-going
- Foods: sweet, heavy (cheesecake), oily, substantial (meat=oily, heavy)
- Colors: white, light-brown
- Season: winter, early spring
- Time of day: 6-10 A.M. or P.M.
- Location in Physiology: chest, low back
- Function in Physiology: structure, strength (immunity), lubrication

Knowing the Doshas, we can start to see the play of creation and how it arises from the underlying field. Knowing this play, knowing these qualities, we can start to understand the qualities of the emotions, and more importantly, how to balance them. We need but know one rule — like increases like. That rule allows us to increase a quality when it is depleted and balance it with its opposite when it is in excess. The intimate connection between mind and body allows us several ways to balance the Doshas' emotions when they are out of balance. That is what the next chapters are all about.

# 7

# UNDERSTANDING VATA EMOTIONS

*"My Vata is vibrant..."*

## *Vital Vata*

In this space we have flow and movement. Vata functions this way with movement and flow and diffusion. The spreading out and flowing nature of the physiology is the influence of Vata. Where all diffuses forth is the purview of Vata. The space element is misunderstood as the ethers. It is, rather, the space in which creation creates. It has its subtle aspect in the ethers, but it is not ether. It is the realm or dimension in which we flow. To have movement we must have space. We must have expansion. To flow and follow forth through the subtle layers of the body is the role of Vata.

Vata has the qualities of space and air. It is dark, cold, expansive, flowing, dispersing, erratic, fast, quick, sudden and ubiquitous. The qualities of Vata are found throughout creation and throughout the body but more importantly in areas that require flow. The flow of the subtle channels, the meridians and *Srotas*, the flow of information in the nervous system — all the flows in the body are where Vata predominates. The most important flow for purification is the colon, and Vata is said to have its seat here, not just because waste flows through this area, but because of the impact of the chakras that are in its area. The first and second chakras both relate to Vata, more the first than the second.

When the first chakra is functioning properly, then the base for space is held. The grounding nature of space is there. The security and foothold for all of the energies to flow forth is founded. Space is the place on which all of the flow and all of emotion is based. Emotion is the movement of energy in the vibratory frequency we call feeling. The vibratory feeling is that movement of the consciousness that creates motion toward an object of desire. To desire this or that we must have the security to go forth in the world and obtain it. When that security is not there, when the first chakra is out of balance, then the fears arise and dominate, and the flow of life is blocked — the path to the goal is hindered. Vata-based fear has this element of walls, of hardness. When the Vata is extreme, the extreme coldness and dryness of Vata hardens things. The personality is rigid, the behavior is compulsive, and the flow is hampered.

Vata is the ruler of the Doshas. It leads all the flows in the body. Pitta cannot leave its seat in the digestive tract without help from Vata causing it to flow elsewhere in the body. Vata rules the flow of life because it sits on the basis of three-dimensional existence — space. Firmly seated in space, the air-like quality of Vata is allowed to diffuse throughout the body, the mind and the emotions.

The movement of emotion is the flow of energy from the vibratory level we call the astral or the *Manomaya Kosha*. It is the flow of all that is to be had from this level or other levels. It is the promulgator, the producer of emotion because it gives rise to the movement and flow of feeling and the communication of the feeling to the awareness. Given the motion that is implied in emotion, this Dosha is key to emotional health. In balanced Vata we have all that is necessary for the proper flow of feeling. Space is clarity, and our clarity of perception of emotion is due to Vata being both balanced and free of Ama. Vata creates clarity. We can see through space when Vata has clear flows in which to operate.

For emotions, Vata creates movement. Movement manifests as excitement, vibrancy and enthusiasm, and most importantly it has the ability to bring liveliness to the feeling level. No other Dosha is as important to keep balanced.

Vata is that aspect of the Unified Field responsible for the construction of time, as time and space are interrelated in the three-dimensional world. Time is crucial in the balance of the individual, and the ancients knew that its improper metabolism was one of the main causes of disease. Abstract as that may seem, simply understand that Vata dominates the other Doshas in terms of its importance for health.

We have described the fundamental elements of Vata, its character, qualities and its import for the emotions. Now it is important to understand the imbalanced Vata emotions, their manifestations and how to rebalance them.

## Frankly Fear

Ama can have us hold emotion within the energy system and eventually within the tissues themselves. It is a major source of disease and illness. Other patterns exist within the emotional body. Imbalance can bring into the energy field a pattern of emotion that dominates the functioning.

In fear we are compelled by the existence of the ego. It is as if the definition were such that all is organized for its survival, for its being. You have this perception of threat, you have the will to survive, and the perception creates the fear and motivates survival. On the emotional level, this survival instinct is pure fear. It is based on the energy coming through the root chakra, and it is always present in those situations where *security* is held most important. It is the Ayurvedic equivalent of Vata imbalance. When this Dosha is misaligned, it brings into the emotional sphere the experience of fear.

Fear perpetuates illusion. The ego sees all as separate, as divided, and its isolation guarantees conflict and the urge for survival. In that state, everything can be feared; everything can be considered a violation or a threat. Fear is the basis for anxiety and numerous diseases — Vata is responsible for more diseases than Pitta and Kapha put together. Ego is a useful structure, but not a real one. It is a mechanism that makes operating in the world most efficient. It is not the purity of the underlying consciousness. Doshas represent impurities in the consciousness of the Unified Field; they are impure because they represent only a part of the whole field.

The divinity in you holds a space free from fear. It represents the truth of you. In acquiring this imbalance you have the possibility of promoting and sustaining *illusion.* The illusion of Vata is the illusion of change. In the changeless, ever-present underlying field, the fluctuations do not alter in any way the field itself. Radio waves do not make any fundamental change in the electromagnetic field that carries the waves. The field remains the field. The nature of Vata is change, but it takes place on the backdrop of the changeless, ever-present, wonderful silence of the Unified Field.

Vata creates the illusion of change and movement. Nothing can disturb the oneness of the Source of Creation — this is why it is called an illusion. In this illusion of change and separateness we create the possibility of fear. We create the notion that there is another besides the Divine. We create that there is something to be feared, that life is finite, that existence can go away, that we can be judged, hurt or shamed. We create this out of the illusion of the ego. We are not that which is separate. The thought patterns we call personality are not the same as the person. We create a separateness and then strive most of our life to bring this back to home.

It is our task to keep this Vata in proper balance. It is the root cause of so many diseases. It is the imbalanced Vata that leads directly to the disease of arthritis, constipation and anxiety.

Our desire to overcome the isolation of the ego is strong; it creates a home away from home. We find convoluted means to gain security in our insecure world. We attach to others and find security in them — for a while. We create the necessity of the other, the dependency on the other to have a sense of distraction from isolation. We find a reprieve in moments of oneness with our beloved, only to be shocked back into the practical world that dictates our continued search for security. Fear is the product of an illusion. It is the product of a mind that does not know the truth of Oneness. It comes when the *experience* of oneness is not available, when the truth of the way to Unity is not imparted as part of the education of the child.

Fear is impossible. When you are lost in the soup of fear, you are completely lost. You can't see the way out of the bowl. You usually can't even see the edge of the bowl, for that matter. But just as you jumped into the soup, you surely can jump out when you realize it is limited. When Vata is severely misaligned then the fear becomes so intense that it is an experience to be avoided — we start to fear the fear itself. Franklin D. Roosevelt stated that we have nothing to fear but fear itself. While that was a political comment on the state of the nation, it points to a deeper truth. Fear keeps us locked in the illusion and creates tremendous suffering. It is the illusion that creates the suffering. It is the illusion that is to be feared.

All it takes to dispel fear and anxiety is one clear moment of perception of the life beyond the ego. If we could just perceive the legions of energy, angels and beings who create the flow of the individual life and see how our individual soul goes on and invites, creates and learns from each event in the life, then we would have no worries. It is no coincidence that those who have had near-death experiences often relate losing their fear of death entirely. With the trauma of an automobile accident most everyone is afraid to drive for a while afterward. But with a near-death experience, the illusion of the impermanence of life is dispelled. Death is no longer feared. With this knowledge, we have the key to dispelling most fears because, ultimately, it is the survival of the ego that is at stake.

We worry what others will think of us if we appear in public in the wrong clothes. We worry about whether our spouse really likes us or not. We worry about money or health. All worry is based on the theory of the ego—the idea that we are separate, that life is random and chaotic, the idea that life is out of our control. When these illusions are accepted as fact, then the possibility of great anxiety, all pervasive and all consuming, comes into existence. Let go of the illusion, and you are freed. Some may say not so, because of the functioning the body. The body is the end stage of the subtle vibrations, programming and patterning. It takes the longest to change. Vata becomes imbalanced and then remains in this locked-in pattern of fear. The body supports the programming and the pattern.

This means that restructuring of the patterning must take place on the level of the body and the mind *simultaneously*. This is the wisdom of Ayurvedic Counseling. We go beyond psychology into the multidimensional aspects of the human being.

Unity is the experience to shake us out of the illusion of the ego. The experience of love is the emotional equivalent of unity. The most potent therapies of Ayurveda to bring about the balance of Vata are based on this nurturing, comforting and caring knowledge of love. Most potent is the warm touch of another's skin against ours. Love is a feared word, all wrapped up in commitment and sexuality, in obligation, guilt and confusion. The word "nurturance" is not so heavily associated. But what balances Vata most is the nurturance that is pure love.

## Love and Bliss Revisited

The separation we had from that which we are was so, so long ago we have no concept, no knowledge of how being separate is an illusion. The heart knows. The heart always unites. It always yearns for unity. It seeks commonality. It seeks to find its complement and merge back into the bliss of Oneness. In the heart we know there is an escape from the torture of the mind, of the ego. In the heart we find freedom, and in love we find ourselves getting lost. So many are afraid of losing themselves in love. We don't really lose ourselves in love. We find our real selves. So many fear they will give up what they have and what they are, so strong is the desire for love, so overwhelming the experience.

What is there to give up? What is there to be lost? Just the trail of concepts of ourselves. Just the cage of the ego... This is what is usually lost in love. But mostly we fear that we will lose control. Fear and control have no place in the temple of love. We are to know this: We each carry a divine spark and will necessarily tread our own divine path, be it sooner or later. If we make perverse sacrifices for the sake of love, like allowing ourselves to be abused, then we have lost in love. But it is not for love that we remain in abusive relationships usually. Usually it is for security. To quell our fears, we talk ourselves into the loss of integrity.

For most of us, though, the fear of losing ourselves in love is unfounded. It is the ego's expression of its need for control. In love, the ego is lost. In love, all sense of separateness and of isolation disappear, and we rejoice in knowing that we are part of something greater, some greater relationship, some greater whole that is so much more than the sum of its parts.

Even the energy flows in the body are affected, in that they are merged. Even the DNA of one enters into another in the physical act of love and does in part incorporate. From the physical, to the energetic, to the emotional, to the spiritual, love creates a ground-shaking transformation of the self into a greater Self. For most people, this transcendental experience is their *only* escape from the confines of the ego, of the limited sense of isolated self. No wonder the physical act of love has such a draw and fascination for the human being. It is not a matter of procreation, as it is for the animals. It is a beautiful release from the prison of the ego.

When the beautiful unity of love becomes confused with sacrifice, then trouble begins. Sacrifice has come to mean a loss, a giving up of something for someone else. Here the ego feels a pain at having to give up something, while at the same time it congratulates itself on being "good" and doing the "loving" thing. The ego pushes on and attempts to give that which it does not have in order to feel good about itself. This is a base understanding of sacrifice that has become the cultural norm and has nothing to do with love.

Sacrifice means to make sacred. You make something sacred by infusing Divinity into it. Then it is Divine and it is sacred. You can only give that which you have. And you can only make something sacred when you have the fullness of the Divinity, the bliss of Being within you. There is no loss in real sacrifice because real love flows effortlessly and only increases in bliss as it expands and flows out to others. It is in fullness that we truly have something to give. When we strain to give, the stress of the strain taints the gift. When we have captured bliss in our awareness, then we have ability to allow love to flow out without loss, creating more and more joy — more and more bliss.

Contact with the field of bliss, the field of pure love, of pure consciousness is the most important way to develop the capacity for true sacrifice. In that experience we shift the mind and infuse it with Being. Then we have the full capability to make anything sacred. Then we can "sacrifice" without loss. In doing for someone else, we know we are doing it for ourselves. For in the experience of the field of pure consciousness, we come to know that we are not our isolated concept of ourselves. We have as much joy in giving to others as we have in giving to ourselves... even more, perhaps, because the joy we experience in the delight of the other is so much more interesting than our own.

In real love, nothing is lost. Only the ego is left behind. That incredible rush, that bliss that we experience when falling in love, when in the arms of another, when knowing the rapture of being cherished and desired by another — that experience can rip us away from the mind's old patterns and plunge us deep into the bliss that resides in the center of our being. All that is lost is the mind's concepts of self and with it, the worries and anxieties and the fears and the sadness.

Capturing the bliss is not reserved for the experience of falling in love. It is available to anyone at any time. It does not depend on finding "the right person." It does not depend on being with someone else. It only requires a way to go deep within, past the mental chatter, past the subconscious mind, past the waves of feelings into the depths of the ocean of pure awareness, pure consciousness, pure bliss.

That is our nature. That is our inheritance. That is what we must connect with in order to have perfect health. And that is where our emotional bliss resides.

## Nurturing Vata

The nonphysical, nonsexual expression of love is to be held in warmth. It's expressed as a warm oil massage done by two attendants in the Ayurvedic system. Yet, it is expressed in so many other ways as self-nurturance — warm, unctuous food prepared by a loving, spiritual cook, warm colors and clothes, comfortable sleep. But the greatest expression of love is found by diving into the field of love itself in deep meditation. Transcending the ego, going beyond thought, image and emotion into the pure consciousness of the Unified Field is a way to contact the field of bliss and love itself.

Self-nurturance on all levels helps to balance Vata. When the emotion of anxiety or fear arises, come back to Self. Come to the Universal. That is the prescription for Vata balancing. This coming back to Self is stepping into the knowledge of the complete Unity of Life, the complete conception of the perfection of the flow of life ... *as it is.* The remembrance, the *Smriti* or memory of the Unity needs to be invoked. The warmth of a mother's touch, the comfort of the womb, the caress of the silence of infinite peace reminds us of the higher reality. All the senses can be used to remind us of who we are. Every association has this feel.

Touch is the sense that is most compelling to remind us of our connection with others. On each level we operate to soothe Vata. On the physical, we need warm oil massage. On the emotional, we need to seek that which "touches" us. On the mental, we need to be exposed to concepts that help us to touch the Divine. On the causal, we need to touch the symbols of unity. And finally on the level of the spiritual, we need to touch the infinite in the deep silence of meditation.

Smell is that sense most connected to the emotional brain. Aroma reminds us of distant memories inherent in us but also inherited by us through the genetic line. It is the power of association that allows the warming scents to remind us of our connection to the Source. Our ability to know and perceive the Unity that underlies can be "remembered" through the intelligence of the complex molecules of an essential oil. Orchestrated to remind us on the emotional or astral plane of our experience of Unity, the proper essence provides the profound experience that eases our anxiety and makes the fear lessen or disappear.

Sight can also be used but not so effectively. It governs more Pitta than Vata, and yet the warming colors, the sight of the expanse of the universe, the beauty of nature can all remind us of something greater than ourselves.

Taste allows us to perceive a warming, soothing influence in the food. But food is not just food. It is the transmitter of subtle vibrations, and if those vibrations belong to a loving, spiritual cook, then the taste conveys the flavor of caring and nurturance — of love.

The sound of Unity is subtle. It occurs when classical music culminates in a final cord, signifying completion, when no one would ever doubt that the piece is finished. Yet, one cannot just listen to the end of a symphony over and over again. Instead, the subtle nature of classical Vedic music (*Gandharva Veda*) is utilized to calm Vata. The microtones are stretched to pull the tones into harmony. This synchronization pulls the nervous system into silence. It settles the mind, pulls it toward unity and the transcendent.

All five senses are able to create this remembrance of Unity. All five senses can be used to balance Vata.

## *Fear — The Final Frontier*

In all this creation, the devil is not in the details. It is in the illusion of separateness. The devil is the fear that motivates and paralyzes. It is the cause of suffering. It is the evil that promotes wars. It is the fundamental human experience at this time. It is to know this fear that makes the experience of Unity such a comfort. In fear we have the stoppage of flow. In fear we have the cessation of life. In fear when have all that is counter to life. This is the power of illusion.

Fear says we cannot survive. Love says life always continues on. Fear says we will suffer. Love says we will be free to be happy.

When fear comes, recognize it and look at it. Feel it. Understand where it resides in the physical. Know it and then let it go. Shift the attention to Unity, to love, to the truth of the perfection of life. We are forever losing ourselves in fear. Lose yourself in Love. This is the final frontier. We are to convert the illusion of separateness into the truth of Love.

Attend to each level of your being when anxiety predominates. Nurture the physical. Rest the body. How can Vata be in balance if you toil and strain and stress the body day in and day out? Rest it. Let it be relaxed. Let it attain deep relaxation. Let it take the sleep that it needs.

Nurture the flows in the body. Yoga asana, Tai chi, Aikido and Qi Gong, if practiced to nourish the energies of the body, will help Vata. Avoid the temptation to turn these into a workout. Stressing and straining the body is the opposite of what Vata calls for. Rekindling the flow of energy, the flow of *prana* through the channels in a very calm and flowing way is what Vata needs.

Nurture the emotions. Attend to them, but do not get lost in them. A father does not stop working every time his child is upset. He comforts and reassures the child but then goes about his work. Comfort the child within. Talk to it and nurture it, but then let it go, and move on to the next task.

Nurture the mind. Turn its focus to love, to positivity, to the oneness of Creation.

Nurture the intuition. Trust it. Allow it to be. Honor it.

Nurture the spirit. Be with it. Meditate and allow all thought to be transcended so that you rest in the peace of spirit, free from fear and anxiety.

The fear comes up. Let it come. Experience it. But don't entertain it with mental analysis and concern. Then let it go. Come back to the Unity that resides under each and every experience. Come back to Unity. Come back to love. Come back to the bliss that is the basis of emotion. Be with that. And know the yoga of emotion.

# *Vacillating Vata — How to Balance Vata Emotions*

When we are anxious and in fear, we vacillate. Vata cannot flow properly. It quakes instead. What to do when the Vata emotions predominate?

Recall that Vata is all about flow. The flow of a river is easily impeded when the river is weak, dried up, tiny. So whatever can aid the flow and increase the volume of the flow will help to keep the river from being thrown off course or obstructed. Remember also that Vata is full of space and will tend to get ungrounded and fly off into diffusion and confusion. Vata needs structure for grounding and for balancing. It needs to be grounded.

Dealing with the Vata emotions is most difficult because of the constant change and shift and the exquisite sensitivity of the human nervous system in a culture designed for bombardment and fatigue. Vata needs nurturing, soothing, grounding and bliss. To rebalance the Vata emotions of fear and anxiety and to move to the pure Vata expressions of enthusiasm and excitement is straightforward.

First, create the supportive physiological environment for the rebalancing process:

- Assure adequate rest. This means throw away the alarm clock, and go to bed early enough to awaken naturally. Attend to any sleep difficulties. (See an Ayurvedic practitioner if you are having sleep disturbance.) Get to bed by 10 P.M.

- Self oil massage daily. (For instructions see the self-education modules at www.newleafayurveda.com). Use sesame oil (or olive oil if there is any irritation with the skin or when using sesame).

- Regular routine. This cannot be emphasized enough. The body can ground more easily when it can predict what is coming.

- Daily asana practice emphasizing floor work, settled or "restorative" poses and practice. Spending several minutes in each pose so that the practice is slow and grounded.

- Eat warm, well-cooked, slightly rich homemade and home-cooked foods.

- Undergo Ayurvedic panchakarma therapy with a 2-person oil massage and rhythmic pouring of oil over the third eye chakra (*Shirodhara*).

Second, create the supportive physical/social environment:

- Seek out people who can be warm, nurturing and supportive.

- Make sure the physical environment is surrounded with pleasant, pleasing, soothing and warming objects, colors and aromas.

Third, re-create the connection with the Source:

- Practice meditation regularly, preferably with an effortless technique of meditation. Nothing is more beneficial for

Vata than meditation. It allows the mind to ground and settle.

- If you don't have a regular meditation practice find instruction in an effortless, mantra-based technique such as Transcendental Meditation (the best, but expensive) or Primordial Sound Meditation or the Art of Living meditation.

Fourth, rebalance the Vata psychology and correct *Pragya Aparad* (mistake of the intellect):

- Calm anxiety with awareness. Stare at the fear or anxiety. Watch it come up, without judgment or analysis, as if you were watching a fire truck go by. Watch how it changes and increases or decreases with each passing moment. Observe where you feel it. Then let it go. It will move or change if you can let it go.

- Recondition the mental-habit patterns. Understand that 90% of everything we worry about never comes to pass. If you are in counseling, ask for help in how to learn that it is only the ego that can be threatened, never the Divine Self. Let go. Allow yourself to live outside of the ego.

- Deal with your Pragya Aparad. Most commonly this is in the form of "I have to be in control or something awful will happen." Explore what aspect of life's flow you are trying to control. When you insist that life must proceed in a certain fashion or that others must perceive you in a certain way in order for you to survive, then you try to control the flow, and the result will always be anxiety and suffering. Replace that attitude with one that expresses that everything is in Divine Order and is happening just as it should.

- Deal with the Pragya Aparad of security. Let your grounding be in your spiritual practice. Let your spiritual life be the security you seek, rather than money or people.

Fifth, integrate and rejuvenate:

- Experience the enthusiasm and increased energy that comes with the freedom, rebalancing the physiology and letting go of the ego.
- Strengthen your connection with the underlying base of life through spiritual practice.
- Take a restful vacation without much travel, and revitalize in the joy of knowing that all is in Divine Order.

You can find out more about how to balance Vata emotions by taking a *Capturing the Bliss Workshop* or attending a seminar on Vedic Counseling, both offered through New Leaf Ayurveda (www.newleafayurveda.com).

*8*

# Playing Through Pitta Emotions

---

*"My Pitta is passionate..."*

## Passionate Pitta

Fire is the essence of human existence. Fire transforms the Divine into the physical and creates our three-dimensional existence. In the fire we are carried to burn all that is impure from our Being so that the clarity of the Divine is expressed in the physical. Pitta is the Dosha of fire. It transforms and metabolizes. It is the essence of the process of creation itself. It creates through transformation. It converts matter to energy. It spiritualizes the material.

Pitta is the flow of life in the fire of love. Passion is the expression of fire of the heart. Passion is that which is necessary to bring in the Divine. It calls forth the energy of the cosmos and focuses its intelligence in creating that which is pictured in the mind. Passion is necessary for manifestation in the physical plane. Desire, intent — these make up the spark, the inspiration that starts the fire and keeps the energy flowing until the goal is reached.

Passion is key in life. All of Nature rises up to support the passion of one who is operating in tune with his or her calling. Do not be deceived. Passion is not reckless desire or an abandonment of responsibility. Passion is the energy of life. What is to be done, whatever is worth doing, is to be done with passion. Life is, ultimately, to be enjoyed. When passion moves, then bliss is in motion. Passion just means giving over to life, to what it has to offer. Restraining one's passion is just putting a damper on life. How can one be healthy and happy with that?

Be in passion. Be in love. Be involved in life, without losing yourself, without losing the higher Self. Let the passion flow through you to the object of the desire. Let the fire burn it up and then come back to the bliss of the eternal Self.

Passion is the fullness of the relative life. The enlightened know that both sides of life are to be lived: the fullness of the transcendent — blissful, peaceful, absolute — and the passion and play of the relative creation where desire (fire) burns and transforms.

Life is so full when it is lived with passion. Life is full and bright when the fire burns brightly. Nothing is so important for success in the world. Nothing is so important for relationship. What is a relationship without passion? It is lifeless. Passion is not sexual. It is intensity of desire. What is a relationship when there is no desire to be with one's partner — to experience, to listen or to help one another? Without passion, it is mechanical and lifeless.

Enlightened passion is the mechanism through which the Divine is made manifest in human form. It is the means through which the energies of the highest frequency are poured into the life. Pitta rules and governs this process. This is the importance of Pitta and its correlate Agni (the fire of digestion). We must transform and metabolize all experience and all emotion, and in that we come to the bliss of life. We relish the experience, and we relish letting it go. We relish integrating into the personality, and we relish letting go of the personality and coming back to the wholeness which is the bliss of the real self, the Higher Self.

All is to be burned in the fire of transformation. That which is not becomes the Ama that creates problems, drama and suffering. So important is Pitta.

All experience is to be transformed into bliss. All experience is to be integrated into the Self. All this transforms and blesses the human experience with the contact and the content of the Divine. In this flow of transformation all becomes possible. Fully metabolizing experience means coming back to the field of all possibilities. From this level all transformations are possible. All can be created. The fire of transforming must be both creative and destructive. Creation creates by transforming the wholeness to limited values and back again to wholeness. In the moment the wholeness takes on other qualities. In the moment the Unity becomes Dosha or impurity and then comes back again to wholeness. This whole process of metabolizing experience is the function, domain and purpose of Pitta.

Fire transforms by destroying one substance and converting it to energy and to ashes. We transform experience by learning how to convert it to bliss and purifying out any of the residual ash through meditation and through the stress-release cycle of sleep. In this manner all experience is converted to higher energies. All experience is to be converted to bliss. It is all our creation for our bliss.

This is important. From the soul level, we create the opportunities, the situations, the challenges. We make agreements with others to present to us the experience we desire *on the soul level.* We agree with other souls to present to us the challenge that we face. We create each aspect of the life and each of our experiences for our learning, for our growth or for our rebalancing some energy or action from the past. This is the hardest to accept. Our enemies are covertly disguised and on the soul level are bringing to us *exactly* what we have asked for. Once we know this, we understand: There are no victims. Understand also this: We are to gain from the experience — the learning, the rebalancing, the impression — and its *sole* purpose is to lead us to greater bliss. The whole process of transformation of experience is to lead to bliss.

Emotional Ama does not simply block the flow of energy. It blocks the transformation process. When incomplete it results in the *absence* of bliss. Ultimately, experience is designed for our greater enjoyment of all things, human and divine.

Processing, transforming means investing a spark into the image and memory of the experience, watching how it flows and grows, how the emotion rises up, and *then* reclaiming the consciousness we have invested in that image, that memory. Coming back to the Self, we know that we have understood the meaning of the experience and are ready for the next. Meaning is obtained in a flash, like knowing the meaning of a symbol, not by analyzing the lines and curves that make up a symbol. We know, "Oh, this is why this is here... This is what this means... This is the learning I have created for myself..." We then let it go and enjoy the bliss of coming back home to our awareness of this moment, with greater clarity and greater consciousness.

A strong fire transforms all that comes in its path. That is why passion is so important. There is an expression, "The greatest sinner is the greater saint." That is because the passion is there; the energy and consciousness are present to be able to make great transformations in oneself and one's society.

Pitta has the qualities of fire — the heat, the intensity, the grounded flowing nature of a fire. It also contains some of the water element and is described as having some oiliness, or some "steam," and hence some fluidity to it. It is pungent, sour, present in foods that would burn when placed on an open blister. It carries with it the power to transform tissue into energy, into awareness.

Pitta is directed. Fire is responsible for sight and the ability to see is necessary to direct one's attention to one's goals. Pitta is direct and goal-oriented. Pitta is able to accomplish all things. Our human desire is a manifestation of Pitta. Desire and passion are akin to each other.

Desire is the beginning of the flow that creates the human life. All of the life is driven by this flow. We have greatly misunderstood this matter. Desire is cast as a trouble-maker, as are most all the beautiful and natural aspects of human life, particularly in the Judeo-Christian cultures. Desire is what organizes and propels the life forward.

It is when life is propelled forward without awareness that desire creates problems. We are to fulfill our desires. When we don't, Pitta becomes imbalanced — the fire does not have the object of the desire to burn, so it burns up something else (the spouse, the IRS, the dog). The Pitta emotions of anger, frustration and jealousy surface when desire is blocked and when awareness is absent.

Pitta is the outpouring of the flow of life into the fire of life. It is the great transformer that awaits the fuel of experience and knows that all will be ultimately returned to the one ocean of bliss. This is the essence of the transformer Pitta. Be forewarned that Pitta is often maligned when in fact it is the lack of awareness that creates problems with fire. Fire and consciousness do not stand apart. A movie screen and the light projected on it are not two separate processes. To make a movie the light must be present to transform and project, and the field of projection must also be present. One without the other makes for nothing. To avoid the light and only want to be in the movie screen of flat awareness is hardly the point. To create a great experience, both the movie projector and the screen are necessary.

Pitta is the fire that gives the light and produces change. That change is in the field of awareness, observable and enjoyable. The transformation is crucial to all creation. It is the act of creation. Pitta burns in that fire of divinity that constantly re-creates life and infinity simultaneously. Life is for us to be involved. The impetus of movement is desire. Without it, movement is directionless and eventually pointless. This is the power of Pitta, to put into motion the desire of our finest intent.

Pitta means to take us to the next level by transforming energy into awareness, by metabolizing experience and by knowing the light that burns brightly within. The Pitta manifestation is fundamental to all creation and to all living beings. Pitta is the light of life that burns for each of us. In that light we see into all of creation. Pitta would be the king of the Doshas were it not for Vata. It is the necessary fire of the transformations of all that is so important in the life.

Pitta is that which sustains our ability to be in human form through the transforming power of digestion. We take in food and transform it to human experience.

In this light of the knowledge of the importance of Pitta, we honor the functions and the passions and the ability to transform our emotional existence into pure consciousness. What we invest in emotions we ultimately must reclaim. It is when the fire is weak that digestion is incomplete, and the investment is more of a loss of energy. Those who are depleted see this in themselves. The emotional energy has been drained away. In love we have all energy. In depression we have none. Pitta is the fire of passion, the fire of digestion, the fire of transformation and the fire of life.

## The Pitta Emotions

Anger, frustration, jealousy — so often these emotions are cited in introductory Ayurveda texts, but they are not only the manifestation of Pitta. They become the topics because they are of such great importance. The purpose of creation is to expand happiness, and the blockage of desire or passion thwarts the whole purpose of life. When that blockage occurs, the energy spews forth as anger, frustration or jealousy, all of which can create destruction in their wake. It is the thwarting of life's purpose that creates such an explosion of energy. And in destroying the desire, life is inevitably destroyed with it. In fulfilling one's desire, the friction does not occur — the heat, the explosion and the debris are all avoided.

Know the positive Pitta emotions of courage, passion and benevolence. These come to the forefront when Pitta is in balance, and passion is directed with the clarity of consciousness and attunement with the needs of the time. Pitta gives us motivation and courage to move forward. It creates the best in us — valor, nobility, generosity. Pitta, when in proper balance, creates the greatest of humanitarians because it gives the passion to take up a worthy cause, the resourcefulness to make it successful, and the organizing ability to ensure it will sustain.

Pitta gives us the passion that is so important in romantic encounters. It gives us the energy to pour our hearts into our relationships and to be committed to another's well-being.

For Pitta to remain in balance, desire and how we relate to it must be elevated to a high state of balance. Desire is an essential part of life. It is to be honored. Suppression of desire, like suppression of love, only can create more problems.

Desire is never the problem. It is the insistence that the desire must be fulfilled that creates the suffering. When we fulfill desire, we can let go of the drive and the energy, and in that letting go process, we come back to the Divine, back to the underlying field of consciousness. It is the strong contact with that field that gives the bliss, the satisfaction that we mistakenly perceive to be in the attainment of the object of our desire. This gives rise to the mistake of attaching our happiness to the fulfillment of our desires. It is not so. The happiness comes from the contact with the bliss of consciousness, not from "getting what we want." We are deceived into the illusion and fall into the trap that comes when we attach our well-being and our happiness to our desires.

The proper technique for desiring is to move with passion and grace toward that which we desire but to let go of the energy after it flows into our awareness. That means we enjoy the desire and the progress we make, but then we return back to our inner-awareness and let go and see if the action manifests in the fulfillment of desire. In letting go we come back to the bliss of the Self. In that all desires are fulfilled, as it is the state of fulfillment. That is the technique for desiring. We don't make a mood of being unattached to desire. We simply learn to enjoy the bliss whether the desire is fulfilled or not. The more we experience this, the more we condition the mind away from the habit of associating happiness with getting what we want.

The wise know that desire finds its fulfillment when we allow Nature to do the work. When we allow ourselves to be in tune with Nature, then desires are spontaneously fulfilled without struggle or stress.

Be full of Pitta to have the power to digest and transform your experience. Be full of Pitta to have the passion to live life to the fullest. Be full of Pitta to allow the nobility and courage to shine forth in service to others. And in the joy of passion, remember to return to the bliss of the Self.

## On Being Pitta-full — What To Do When Pitta is Imbalanced

When Pitta runs too high and the feelings of irritability and frustration arise, then it is time to focus on rebalancing Pitta. From the standpoint of Vedic Counseling this requires adjustments on several levels:

First, create the supportive physiological environment for the rebalancing process:

- Assure that rest is adequate.
- Cool off with a cooling daily oil massage with olive, sunflower or coconut oil. (For instructions, see the self-education modules at www.newleafayurveda.com.)
- Practice daily yoga asana that is cooling and without a strong goal-orientation.
- Undergo Panchakarma therapies that eliminate heat from the body, such as *Virechana* (laxative therapy) and a cooling *Shirodhara* (pouring oil over the forehead continuously with a cooling oil).
- Avoid spicy, vinegary, acid-producing foods (such as tomatoes, beef).

Second, create the supportive physical/social environment:

- Pitta gets so focused and wrapped up in the goal that it ignores taking time to smell the roses. What Pitta needs most is love. This is often the motivation deeply underlying the incessant activity. Being around people who are laid-back and loving is what is needed to give Pitta a break.

- Stop overworking and overdoing.

Third, recreate the connection with the Source:

- Nothing is as cooling to the mind as meditation. Consider regular meditation preferably with an effortless technique of meditation. Meditation allows a clearer perspective. It takes away the attachment to *having* to meet the goal and allows one to proceed to greater success with less effort and attachment.

- If you don't have a regular meditation practice find instruction in an effortless, mantra-based technique.

- Assure that sleep is not disturbed. If you are having long awakenings in the night, then see the self-education modules at www.newleafayurveda.com.

Fourth, rebalance the Pitta psychology and deal with Pragya Aparad (mistake of the intellect):

- Decrease intensity by slowing the pace of speech and thought.

- Deal with the Pragya Aparad that mistakenly insists that one's worth can be rated. Understand that we are of value solely by the fact that we are all an expression of the Divine.

- Let go of judging and measuring. "Judge not lest ye be also judged."

- If you are in counseling, learn the process of playing with desire, rather than letting it control you.

- Learn the technique of coming back to the source of contentment, coming back to the Self. This is the processing of desiring and then letting go in *each moment.*

- Focus on love.

Fifth, integrate and rejuvenate:

- Plan a day each week where there is no schedule.

- Get outside in nature each day. Nature connects us with something bigger than ourselves, our goals and our passions.

You can find out more about how to balance Pitta emotions by taking a *Capturing the Bliss Workshop* or attending a seminar on Vedic Counseling, both offered through New Leaf Ayurveda (www.newleafayurveda.com).

## *9*

# COPING WITH KAPHA EMOTIONS

*"My Kapha is king..."*

## *Kapha Dosha*

There is only one key to Kapha: The essence of physical life is necessary through a physical body. Kapha is this physical essence. It is the presence of this physicality, this ability to add structure that is feared because of the fear of obesity. Thus, Kapha's true nature is often misunderstood. Kapha's key is water. Water is the flow, which flows with life, flows with emotion. Flowing into one another in all ways, we simulate the unity that exists in higher consciousness and are reminded of unity, of love. The flow of Kapha is the flow of water. The emotions are of the water — they are of Kapha as much as of any of the Doshas. When they are stuck, it is Kapha that slows them and makes them sticky. The key, though, to understanding Kapha is to understand the nature of water.

Water is the essence of physical life. It is the essence of emotional life. Water trickles wherever it can. Take two puddles of water and mix them together, and you have no memory of two, just one large pool of water. A stagnant pool is toxic. Without flow, then all life goes. Without being full, the energy weakens. A dried-up pool has little flow. We are to flow in and out of the pool of emotion and allow them to come and go like the waves on an ocean.

Pushed out of awareness, taught to avoid and suppress feeling, we stop the flow of emotion, and the water becomes stagnant and toxic. That is the message of Kapha for the emotions. Let the water element be present — let it flow — and the physical body will be so much healthier.

Kapha is king because it is the base from which we find the waters of emotion. The symbol for emotion in the Tarot is water that is held in the suit of cups. It is the flowing forth of emotion that gives Kapha its import. However, in this, remember the highest emotion is love. Kapha in proper balance is all about love. It shows and radiates a jovial acceptance, a loving attitude and a warm embrace. It accepts all as if it were rolling off the bliss of the love and joy that fills the room with its largeness and fullness.

Kapha has that Santa Claus effect. It is warm, inviting, loving, and forever patient and kind. That is its strength: its grounded settledness in the peace and understanding of the base of life. In that, Kapha finds its place in the world of activity and dynamism. Its base serves to buffer the activity all-consuming in so many lives. Above all, kapha is kind.

Kapha is responsible for structure and for strength (and immunity). It is the physical base. But on the emotional level, it is the actual vibration of emotion that is the vibration of the water element of Kapha. Stable and full of structure, it gives grounded emotional expression.

When Kapha is out of balance, it gets stuck. It gives rise to attachment, depression, loss of motivation and overall feeling of stuckness. It gives rise to excessive sleep, as the joy of life is gone too easily, and there is no real reason for being awake for the imbalanced Kapha. It is easy to rebalance, though, and few remain in this imbalanced state for long.

Kapha is sticky. It attaches itself at times to things and people in a way that creates dependency and staleness. Kapha, composed of earth and water, provides the ground, the base upon which the water can flow. Water will disperse into the space of Vata in 100,000 droplets without any earth. It will be dispersed into steam in the fire of Pitta and have no place to rest. It is the earth element that serves as the basis for the emotional grounding that is necessary to feel and be comfortable in the realm of feelings. Kapha supplies both. That is why it is the king of the Doshas as far as emotion is concerned. Vata is the queen of the Doshas, responsible for flow and movement and clarity. Pitta is the noble minister who gives forth generously for the benefit of all.

When we understand Kapha we find its essence in the balanced state of love. It is here that we can reside and find our base — not in the love of a particular individual, nor in receiving love, but rather in experiencing the love that exists within us, as our base. Our basis, our foundation is the underlying field of consciousness which must flow to create us, to create everything in manifest creation. Love is consciousness in motion. It is the essential nature of consciousness, and we are it. We are essentially love. When we experience that deep within, then we know. We are it. Everything is it, and it is all there is.

The foundation of Kapha's love forms the underpinnings of the structure of all emotion. Its bliss is the goal we seek with each desire. Its loss is what we grieve when we experience any loss. Its essence is what we are missing when fear arises, and we fail to perceive the loving nature of the Divine.

Keep your waters flowing. Keep them pure and love will be yours.

## My Kapha is Clogged — What To Do When Kapha Becomes Imbalanced

When Kapha is imbalanced, there is a stuckness in the emotional field. Attachment, dependency, even greed can result.

Most commonly, though, there is a loss of emotion, a depression that zaps all motivation. When Kapha is out of balance and the negative side of Kapha expresses itself on the emotional level, taking the following measures can help:

First, create the supportive physiological environment for the rebalancing process:

- Daily yoga asana practice that is vigorous, warming, and that even creates a good sweat can be very valuable. In addition, there should be some part of the yoga asana practice that allows one to turn inward and discover when the emotions are being stuck and held in the body, so that this emotional Ama can be released.

- Undergo Panchakarma therapies that eliminate Ama from the body, such as *Udvartana* (herbal scrubs), *Swedana* (steams), Virechana (laxative therapy), *Basti* (medicated enema), and *Nasya* (nasal inhalations).

- Take a lighter diet with spicy, pungent foods, and lots of bitter taste (greens, salads, etc.).

- Do a liquid diet (thick soups, thick liquids) one day a week.

Second, create the supportive physical/social environment:

- When we are stuck, it is good to be around people who are dynamic and motivated. Seek out successful Pitta types and spend more time with them.

- Lighten up your physical environment by throwing out any old clothes, papers or books and removing all clutter.

Third, recreate the connection with the Source:

- Nothing is as effective in removing over-attachment as is meditation. Consider regular meditation, preferably with an effortless technique of meditation. Meditation takes away the attachment to *having to have* the object of one's desire.

- If you don't have a regular meditation practice find instruction in an effortless, mantra-based meditation technique.

Fourth, rebalance the Kapha psychology and deal with Pragya Aparad (mistake of the intellect):

- Deal with the Prayga Aparad that mistakenly insists that love comes from outside of us. It is not the person we depend on who is the source of love. They are there to remind us of the love waiting to be awakened within us.

- If you are in counseling, deal with any boundary issues that keep you from being separate and autonomous and keep you in co-dependency with others.

- If you are feeling depressed, understand that one positive thought will counter the energy of 10 negative thoughts.

- Focus on joy. List those things that have brought forth joy in the past, and try to engage in at least one of these activities each day.

Fifth, integrate and rejuvenate:

- Get physically moving each day, preferably out in nature.
- Travel to a place that brings you joy, and enjoy the love that can come through change, movement and shifting of place.

You can find out more about how to balance Kapha emotions by taking a *Capturing the Bliss Workshop* or attending a seminar on Vedic Counseling, both offered through New Leaf Ayurveda (www.newleafayurveda.com).

# *10*

## RELATIONSHIPS AND THE TREASURE WITHIN

---

## *Relationships and the Doshas*

Out of the bliss of the Unified Field, the play of creation emerges with each Dosha expressing its role. From the peaceful bliss, moves and stirs this love that creates all creation, and each Dosha has its moment on the stage before it returns back to wholeness.

In the glory of Vata, Kapha is motivated by her enthusiasm to move and join. In his solid stability, she finds security and comfort.

In the glory of Pitta, Vata finds warmth and generosity, and Vata gives back a playfulness that lightens the stern seriousness of Pitta.

In the glory of Kapha, Pitta finds ease and relaxation and gives back intensity, energy and drive that overcome the cool sluggishness of Kapha.

And then when Vata meets Vata, there is an endless play of banter, talking, laughter and excitement that leads everywhere and nowhere and just revels in its exuberance.

And when Kapha meets Kapha, the love and joy just flow and flow and flow.

And when Pitta meets Pitta, there is the passion of the gods whose intensity mere mortals only dream of.

In each of the Doshas the glory of love expresses itself in the play of relationship and provides infinite opportunities for appreciation, for growth and for coming back to the wholeness of the Self that underlies everything. In engaging in the play, we offer our essence and come to embrace our differences and awaken finally to discover that behind each difference, underlying each emotion is the bliss of pure love.

And so we go out and come back again and again to the infinite Absolute Divinity that is creation — that is who we are. And in experiencing who we really are, we discover infinite love.

In the flow of life, we stop to see how we can fill the void within and cling to some view of ourselves that the mind creates. The flow of nature through us, through our unique offering to the world is stopped. We reach for that which is seemingly so vital to our happiness. We have no way to know the blueprint that the Divine has placed in the lap of our soul. We wander forth away from ourselves and away from Nature. Any flow we stop becomes a possibility for pain. Stop the flow of blood with a tourniquet, and soon the limb begins to hurt. Stop the flow of energy in an acupuncture channel, and soon a sharp pain results. Stop the flow of emotion, and an end to bliss is the result.

Life flows. Nature flows. We shape the flow with our unique character. Whether that character is the classic of a thin, airy Vata type or whether our mental/emotional nature is of one type while our body manifests other characteristics — it does not matter. What we are given — the gifts we bring, the talents we possess the possibilities we have within, the potential we are developing... It all is part of the flow of Nature.

Ayurveda recognizes that in understanding the flow, the variation in creation, we understand the play of creation, and we are to provide to one another all the variety and happiness that relationship can bring.

## *The Treasure Within*

In this writing, we come to know the treasure within — the treasure of the ages, the hidden one, the one without a second. What is it that is so precious, yet so hidden? Our awareness. Our consciousness. Consciousness is the treasure. It gives us our life. It pulls us to our destiny. It allows us to experience our human existence. It creates. In knowing this, we become co-creators with the Higher Power. Consciousness sets up the myriad of connections that come to one's aid once one has committed to an intention. It is responsible for all sorts of unforeseen happenings and circumstances. It is responsible for serendipity and synchronicity. It is responsible for "luck."

Inside the treasure is where all success resides, where all fulfillment resides, where every desire has the potential to be fulfilled. Inside of us resides the fountain of youth, the immortal aspect of our nature, our liveliness.

Inside resides our health. Consciousness heals. It unites and *is* our liveliness. It reconnects the fragmented array of cells to some greater organization and brings intelligence to an otherwise disjointed and chaotic collection of cells. It brings warmth and nurturance. It brings wholeness. It shines on the dark spaces and brings light.

Consciousness brings love. It is in essence love in motion. It is the love that is beyond male and female, beyond mother and child that is the essence of the Divine. It brings all this forth to create healing, if you only will allow it and not cloud it and overwhelm it. It is the light of love in our life.

Consciousness is the treasure that brings treasure. It is the source of all growth in creation and the container of every template that exists for the structured growth of every living creature and every human soul. It is the source of abundance. It is what creates wealth. It is what real wealth is. It is only necessary to understand the principles of consciousness in order to understand how to manifest abundance. Understanding the treasure within, we connect to the mine that contains all treasure, and we become owners of it.

In knowing awareness we know the simple truth. In knowing consciousness we know all that is capable of being known. We know the source of all knowledge, the structure where all knowledge resides. And we know that which perceives knowledge, that which is aware of it and that which experiences it and knows that it knows. Consciousness is the source of knowingness.

It is magnetic and allows the universe to draw to us that perfect experience we need for our learning and rebalancing. It is perfect in its organization and in its execution. It is perfection.

Consciousness is that which brings the experience of happiness, of peace, of bliss and of fulfillment. In knowing consciousness, we experience the source of bliss, the origin of happiness and the home of fulfillment.

Consciousness brings life, health, healing, love, knowledge, abundance, immortality, happiness and fulfillment. It is so important and so little-known. So what resides in you? All knowledge — the source of healing, all love — the source of all abundance, immortality, happiness and life itself. Yet, so well-hidden is this treasure that it goes ignored. It is the riddle of the ages, how the source of all that is important in life can be so well-hidden.

Better not to ponder the riddle; rather, just develop consciousness. Be in the light of consciousness.

How to know the treasure? How to know consciousness? Guiding the mind to thoughts of spirituality does not give the experience of consciousness. It is impossible to know consciousness with the constant distraction of the mind and the senses. To know it we must sit beyond thought and beyond sensation and become familiar with it in its purity without the coverings and trappings of mind, emotions and sensation. This is real meditation.

When a healer moves energy and heals the physical body, a part of consciousness is known. When the intuitive flash appears, direct knowing gives an experience of part of consciousness and the knowledge it contains. When we fall in love and we feel such bliss, then another aspect of consciousness is known. But only in knowing consciousness by itself can we simultaneously experience all love, all bliss, all knowledge and perfect health. Know the treasure within, and know the Divinity that you are, and let your love flow forth in all ways.

# *Resources*

For more information about Ayurveda, its application to daily life and its insight into emotions, please visit the New Leaf Ayurveda website at <u>www.newleafayurveda.com</u>.

Dr. Dugliss offers the *Capturing the Bliss Workshop,* seminars on Vedic Counseling and other training programs throughout the year. More information and schedules can be found on the New Leaf Ayurveda website.